Designs for Churches
and Chapels

Copyright © 2010   Spire Books Ltd and Christopher Webster

CIP data:
A catalogue record for this book is available from the British Library
ISBN 978-1-904965-29-9

Designs for Churches and Chapels

W.F. Pocock

First published 1819

WITH AN INTRODUCTION BY

CHRISTOPHER WEBSTER

Spire Books Ltd

PO Box 2336, Reading RG4 5WJ
www.spirebooks.com

William Fuller Pocock (1779-1849) was a late Georgian, London-based architect who, enterprisingly, in 1819 published his pioneering *Designs for Churches and Chapels of various dimensions and styles; consisting of Plans, Elevations and Sections: With Estimates, also Some Designs for Altars, Pulpits, and Steeples*. His publisher was Josiah Taylor 'at the Architectural Library'. The book was reprinted without any changes whatsoever – save the date on the title page – in 1823 and again in 1835 by which time the business had passed to Martin Taylor, probably Josiah's nephew. The present facsimile is taken from the 1835 edition.

It was the first English pattern book to be devoted to the subject of church and chapel design and its timing was significant, coming in the wake of the 1818 Church Building Act, which was widely and correctly expected to generate huge numbers of ecclesiastical projects. However, the book was also equally useful to Nonconformists and much of the content deals with the design of chapels. Furthermore, many of the plates could have been adopted by any of the Protestant denominations.

Architects were the obvious market for the book, but Pocock's Preface stresses that it would also be of real value to those proposing to instigate a church- or chapel-building project. He therefore lays out a set of basic principles as to how clients could best prepare a brief for their architect. Pocock's book remained the only practical guide to the subject until the wave of Ecclesiologically-inspired publications in the 1840s. It is a remarkable book and an invaluable summary of current thinking on its subject on the eve of the biggest church building programme since the Middle Ages.

–

Introduction

In 1827 the patience of the churchwardens of Glossop in Derbyshire reached breaking point. Five years and much money had by then been devoted to a bungled rebuilding of their medieval church that they had placed in the hands of the minor Sheffield surveyor Edward Drury. In desperation, they called in the experienced ecclesiastical architect Robert Dennis Chantrell, who travelled nearly 40 miles from Leeds over the Pennine hills to inspect the work. Chantrell noted the old building had been 'taken down and rebuilt most injudiciously and is in very bad taste' and proposed extensive remedial work. In defence of their earlier patronage, the wardens explained 'church architects are not much found in this area.'[1] It would indeed have been optimistic to imagine an architect experienced in rebuilding a Gothic church could be found in this remote town, but even more remarkable was the earlier case of the new church for Travis Street, near the heart of Manchester. In 1820, the Commissioners of the 1818 Church Building Act had awarded the town funds for a huge building and, as happened in almost all the northern counties, the local committee wanted Gothic. Plans were obtained from three of the principal Manchester architects – Richard Lane, John Palmer and Thomas Wright. All were accomplished designers, but none could satisfy the Commissioners and their architectural advisors in London. Subsequently, there were discussions with Francis Goodwin and Thomas Rickman, yet even this pair failed to please the Commissioners' Architects' Committee. Exasperated, the chairman of the local committee wrote to London, 'as our best talent has failed to please you again [we apply to you] for copies of any plans you may have already approved or of such parts of plans as may enable the Architects here to complete their designs to your satisfaction.'[2]

What these two cases reveal is that while there were funds available in the post-Waterloo (1815) period to build or rebuild churches – both from local fund-raising or government initiatives – the explicit determination of those charged with organising the projects for Gothic structures often ran well ahead of the architectural profession's ability to provide suitable designs. And a Classical scheme that would be universally praised could not be guaranteed either; generally, designers were much more confident when asked for a 'Grecian' – that is, a Greek or Roman – composition, but the critics too were on more comfortable ground and when so moved, could condemn with both confidence and authority.[3] Clearly, what was needed was a reliable pattern book. The extent to which Pocock's *Designs for*

Fig. 1. George E. Hamilton, *Designs for Rural Churches*, John Weale, 1836, Plate III. Before the 1840s, this was Pocock's only competition. It contains twelve designs shown in perspective and then four largely unrelated plans. Most, like this, are of little practical value to the architectural profession.

Churches and Chapels, the subject of this facsimile, succeeded in filling this gap in the publishing market will be examined later. However, before that, it needs to be considered in the context of the Georgian architectural book trade.

William Fuller Pocock (1779-1849) published *Designs for Churches and Chapels of various dimensions and styles; consisting of Plans, Elevations and Sections: With Estimates, also Some Designs for Altars, Pulpits, and Steeples* in 1819. It was reprinted without any changes whatsoever – save the date on the title page – in 1823 and 1835. The first edition was launched precisely twenty years before the birth of the Cambridge Camden Society,[4] an event which would, for ever, change the form of Anglican churches and the worship they contained. It was also one of only two books devoted to the design of buildings for worship to appear in these two decades, decades which witnessed a remarkable quantity of church building activity. The other book, G.E. Hamilton's *Designs for Rural Churches*, contained a series of designs which were largely inept and poorly illustrated (**Fig. 1**).[5] By the time of its publication in 1836, the plates were hopelessly old-fashioned. Other, more general, pattern books in this period usually had, at most, a pair of ecclesiastical designs, alongside schemes for assembly rooms, libraries, gas works and markets, and several had none at all; Pocock was in a unique position.

This essay will examine his book, its usefulness and the context for its publication; perhaps most interestingly, it will consider the question of the extent to which the book trade assisted in the dissemination of material useful to the architect seeking

Fig. 2. Bristol, Holy Trinity, Trinity Road (T. Rickman and H. Hutchinson, 1829–31), loosely based on King's College Chapel, Cambridge, a popular medieval model for post-Waterloo churches.

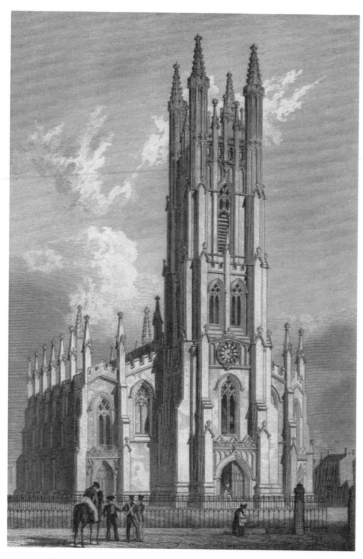

Fig. 3. Manchester, St George, Hulme (Francis Goodwin, 1826-8), one of the more impressive examples of an early Commissioners' church. (*Lancashire Illustrated, 1831, opp. p. 90.*)

to understand Gothic as a prelude to the production of an effective ecclesiastical composition in this then largely unfamiliar style.

In relation to the best of the churches that appeared in the 1820s, from the offices of Rickman (**Fig. 2**), Barry or Goodwin (**Fig. 3**), Pocock's offerings might seem idiosyncratic. However, the book is a remarkable document: the first publication ever to appear on the subject of the design of new churches and chapels and for seventeen years, the only one in existence; a book that had a profound effect on North American church and chapel building; and a compelling snapshot of current thinking on its subject in the heady days of 1819. It was published only months after the passing of the 1818 Church Building Act, and on the eve of what was probably the largest programme of English church building since the Middle Ages, but before any construction had been undertaken, and before the standard type of 'Commissioners' churches' had been established.

The book trade and architectural style

At least as far back as the first volume of Colen Campbell's *Vitruvius Britannicus* in 1715, one can trace the way in which publications helped lead changes in architectural fashion. Campbell's book set out the case for abandoning the 'licentious [and] extravagant' Baroque in favour of the style of Palladio 'who has exceeded all who have gone before him'.[6] Robert and James Adam used their *Works in Architecture* to promote 'the beautiful spirit of antiquity' in 1778,[7] while a decade earlier, James Paine's *Plans* cautioned against too great a reliance on the 'despicable ruins of ancient Greece'[8] to foster his alternative. And by the opening years of the nineteenth century, a succession of books attempted to satisfy the current vogue for the picturesque in architecture. What all these – and many other – publications demonstrate is that a judiciously compiled book could achieve real success by establishing or riding the crest of a new fashion: its letterpress could legitimise stylistic innovation, and the plates would reveal how it could best be translated into functional buildings. That no one apart from Pocock attempted to capitalise on the huge post-Waterloo church building program – especially by providing effective Gothic designs – seems, in the context of earlier publishing successes, an obviously missed opportunity.

Writing in 1960, John Summerson identified those churches that were the product of the 1818 Church Building Act as sufficiently numerous to form one of the four 'major church-building episodes … since the close of the Middle Ages.'[9] They were indeed, and if to the buildings promoted by the Commissioners are added those new churches that were financed by other means, then this quarter century was truly remarkable for the sheer quantity of accommodation that was constructed. How many new or rebuilt Anglican churches were there? A precise calculation is difficult, but the Customs and Excise 'Drawback Account',[10] published in 1838 and covering the period from 1817 to March 1838, records that returns were made on 225 new churches promoted by the Church Building Commission and probably 101 other new churches – mainly rebuilding of earlier structures – funded by alternative means, usually a single patron or group of subscribers. In total, at least 326 churches were built in this twenty-one-year period.[11] No one seems to have attempted to calculate the number of Non-conformist building projects in the post-Waterloo period, but they were certainly more numerous than those for the Anglicans. What is clear is that in the quarter century that followed Waterloo – conveniently terminated by the birth of Ecclesiology and a new generation of books that illustrated and promoted medieval churches as suitable models for emulation – there were literally hundreds of jobs available for an architect able to rise to the challenges that the design and erection of a church or chapel engendered. Any book of sound, adaptable designs – even if they were largely unremarkable – would surely have been eagerly bought by the profession. Pocock had an additional market in mind: 'Ministers' and others intending to 'promote' church and chapel building, and he discusses in some detail how such persons could consider in broad terms what sort of building would satisfy their needs, how they should embark on the building process and the best ways of managing the building trades.[12]

William Fuller Pocock

The important facts of Pocock's life and work can be found in a useful essay on the Pocock family,[13] in Colvin's *Biographical Dictionary*,[14] and there is some additional material in the 'Dictionary of Methodism'.[15] Interestingly, none makes more than a passing reference to *Designs for Churches and Chapels*. A summary of the biographical details will suffice here. He grew up in London, the son of a 'joiner, carpenter and maker of patent extensible furniture'. Although initially apprenticed to his father, Pocock was determined to become an architect and in 1796 enrolled as a pupil of Charles Beazley (*c*.1760-1829), a minor London architect; in 1801 he was an assistant to Thomas Hardwick Jnr (1752-1829),[16] a leading – but conservative – late-Georgian church designer, perhaps best remembered as the two times-restorer of Inigo Jones's fire-damaged St Paul's, Covent Garden. Pocock was, according to his son, 'a meticulous, hard-working man, reserved in manner and "scrupulously clean and neat" in his appearance.'[17] His integrity, efficiency and reliability would explain the numerous surveyorships which were the bread and butter work of his office, and in addition he secured some thirty known commissions before retirement in 1843. The buildings – although varied in style and function – are typical of the work likely to be directed at this time towards the profession's second division, and Colvin concludes he was 'competent but unremarkable, his best work being in the Greek Doric style.' Significantly, the list of his works reveals no churches at all and just one chapel by 1819, although in the Introduction to *Designs for Churches,* Pocock claims that 'the circumstances in which I have been placed for many years past, having led me to study Ecclesiastical Architecture, which is not quite in the general line of practice … I may, therefore, without vanity, hope that I am not entirely destitute of that information which is necessary for constructing buildings of this description.'[18] He was an active member of the Wesleyan movement and while he is not recorded as the recipient of its pre-1819 architectural patronage,[19] as a prominent member of its community, he must have visited many of its chapels and noted the variety of plans its buildings contained, a point to which we will return.

There is another aspect of his career that should be noted here: his work as an author. Pocock's published three pattern books: *Architectural Designs for Rustic Cottages, Picturesque Dwellings, Villas etc,* in 1807 (reprinted 1819 and 1823); *Modern Furnishings for Rooms …* , 1811 (again in 1823 and 1837); and finally *Designs for Churches and Chapels*.[20] Three pattern books by an architect who can reasonably be described as 'unremarkable' is significant, and all three generated reprints over many years. It is, perhaps, not unreasonable to conclude that, for their author, the rewards of authorship were not only *via* the royalties they brought, but additionally for the business they generated; in both *Architectural Designs* and *Churches and Chapels*, Pocock makes a point of inviting potential clients to visit his office. Perhaps he was instrumental in promoting the reprints. Following the success of his first two ventures, he seems to have taken the initiative with the third by anticipating that the 1818 Church Building Act and the formation of what became the Incorporated Church Building Society the same year would produce countless commissions to build or extend churches alongside the already burgeoning chapel building activities.

The preparations for publication.

Ambitiously, Pocock tried to appeal to three relatively distinct markets: those seeking designs for plain Nonconformist chapels, and for Anglican churches in either the Classical or Gothic styles. The book is completed by a series of exclusively Classical designs for spires, 'Altar-pieces' and pulpits.

A precise categorisation of the designs by denomination is problematic as 'chapel' might equally be used for a Nonconformist establishment or for something below the rank of a parish church for the Church of England. And since all the designs were adaptable, perhaps this sort of analysis is redundant. Nevertheless, it would seem reasonable to conclude that the book's fourteen different compositions probably comprise six Classical Nonconformist chapels, four Classical Anglican churches, three Gothic Anglican ones, and a Gothic design that might have been intended for either side of the religious divide.

How might Pocock have set about compiling the book's contents? Like the authors of other pattern books, he would have been keen to inform the readers where a design had been executed; since this happened only in the case of the Ranelagh Chapel, Sloane Square, London (1818, demolished 1870), it can reasonably be concluded the remaining thirteen designs were produced specifically for publication. What were their likely sources? As an established author, he would have owned at least a small library of architectural books, and while they would have offered him little in the way of direct models, recent books on the Classical past could have offered less obvious inspiration, as we shall see.

Pocock's Preface is not without interest. He tells us he had 'studied ecclesiastical architecture'.[21] Immediately one imagines earnest sketching trips around the country's great cathedrals and myriad parish churches, although the text suggests his interests, which were essentially pragmatic, were not primarily concerned with stylistic niceties, but with current issues of efficient planning. Thus, the starting point for 'Ministers and others … desirous' of building is to 'have some specific outline of

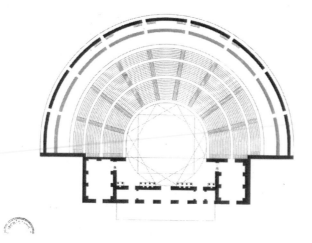

Fig. 4. 'The Theatre of Herodes Atticus at Athens' from William Wilkins, *The Civil Architecture of Vitruvius*, Longman et al, 1812, pl. 7, perhaps the inspiration for Pocock's Plate 3. *(Leeds Library.)*

a plan ... There are two points to which the attention should be principally directed in the building of Churches – the *number it is necessary to accommodate, and the expense that will probably attend it.* [Here and below, the italics are Pocock's.] I have therefore, in the descriptions of these Designs, given [answers to these questions] ... I have purposefully avoided every thing that is splendid and magnificent; and have studied to produce such Designs only, as are plain, suitable to the purpose, and at the least possible expense'.[22] Nevertheless, he had been 'attentive to elegance, by avoiding everything that is mean and vulgar in appearance.'[23] He then demonstrates his credentials as a historian and in a mere 250 words considers the merits of some of the key religious buildings of the previous two millennia – including, remarkably, Santa Sophia in Constantinople – before concluding that they are 'not so well calculated for the simplicity and purity of Protestant worship. [For] Protestant or Reformed Churches' the salient point is '*the most convenient method of seating the greatest number of persons to hear distinctly the voice of the reader and preacher*'[24] and while hardly a radical idea – Wren had made the same observation a hundred years earlier[25] – this is central to our understanding of Pocock's philosophy as a designer.

'The only buildings of antiquity' that he identified as 'authorities' in church and chapel planning are theatres, and those of the Greeks are more appropriate models than those of the Romans, an idea gleaned, perhaps, from William Wilkin's recent *The Civil Architecture of Vitruvius* (**Fig. 4**).[26] But the most efficient arrangement of all, 'preferred [by] gentlemen in the habit of public speaking [is the] parallelogram, with a portion of a circle at the extremity.'[27] Pocock was an advocate of galleries to maximise accommodation 'to allow the preacher's voice to be heard in every part', and even sanctioned a second gallery for while they gave the church 'too much the appearance of our theatres', we should not be 'obliged to give up the convenience on that account'.[28]

So much for his general principles, but what recent buildings might he have sought out as models? As far as Nonconformist buildings are concerned, late-Georgian London saw a considerable increase in numbers and as a Wesleyan, he would have been personally familiar with many of them. Certainly he knew Wesley's Chapel on City Road, where he worshipped with his family and which his father helped to build.[29] Its plain, red-brick façade and semi-circular-topped windows was much copied. The man now widely regarded as 'the outstanding figure in Methodist building'[30] in the early nineteenth century was William Jenkins (c.1763-1844) who operated as both a minister and architect. He was based in London, was not much older than Pocock and the two would surely have moved in the same circles. Jenkin's Wesleyan Chapel in St Peter's Street, Canterbury (1811) (**Fig. 5**) is entirely typical of late-Georgian, sparingly ornamented chapels; it also has much in common with some of the models in Pocock's book. By 1819, a discernable pattern of design had been established: a rectangular, galleried body with a pair – or more – of entrances at the street end, dressed in a (usually) plain Classical style. The Wesleyan Chapel in Calderwood Street, Woolwich (1815-16) is a standard example – and

Fig. 5. Canterbury, Wesleyan Chapel, St Peter's Street (William Jenkins, 1811), a typical example of pre-Pocock plain chapel Classicism. (*Reproduced by permission of English Heritage, NMR*)

Fig. 6. William Thomas, Surry Chapel, London, 1783. Aquatint engraving by Augustus Pugin and W.J. White after Rudolf Ackermann 'Interior of Surry Chapel, Southwalk in London, 10 May 1812'. (*Guildhall Library, London, 19469.*)

not unlike those from Jenkins' office – as was the Independent Claremont Chapel in Pentonville Road, Islington (1818-19), and perfectly timed to attract Pocock's attention. In the provinces, Lendal Chapel, York, by the prolific chapel architect J.P. Pritchett (1816) has much in common with the façade of Pocock's Ranelagh Chapel of 1818, illustrated in the book. However, various congregations were more innovative and before 1819, Nonconformity had an impressive record of exploring alternative plans. The Octagon Chapel, Norwich (1750s),[31] the octagonal Unitarian Chapel, Paradise Street, Liverpool (1791),[32] the vast Surry Chapel (1783) (**Fig. 6**) and the oval First Presbyterian Church in Belfast (1781-3) are just some of the many successful alternatives to the parallelogram. Indeed, the *Minutes of the Methodist Conference* of 1770 specifically recommended the octagon as 'best for the voice, and on many accounts more commodious than any other',[33] and John Wesley recorded his enthusiasm for Belfast's arrangement after preaching there in 1789.[34]

While the Nonconformists had sought to extend their influence by an aggressive programme of chapel building, construction by the Church of England had been sluggish, especially during the long war with France and its recent churches were, on the whole, 'architectural oddities' according to Summerson.[35] The period's major architects were not much concerned with ecclesiastical projects and there were only limited examples for Pocock to study. Interestingly, his former masters Beazley and Hardwick had rather more engagement with this branch of practice than most, and Hardwick had produced a number of new churches in the 1790s and 1800s, either during, or just before Pocock's arrival in his office. Subsequently, he must have watched with interest the construction of Hardwick's St Marylebone Parish Church (1813-17), the most prominent new church of the period immediately prior to the publication of his book (**Fig. 7**). However, Hardwick's 1810s churches, with their impressive, but orthodox – and expensive – porticos seem not to have much interested Pocock; his brand of Classicism was more idiosyncratic and a church that was likely to have been admired by him was S.P. Cockerell's St Martin's, Outwich, London (1796-8) which, as we shall see later, shares a number of features with Pocock's particular approach to composition (**Fig. 8**). James Spiller's St John's, Hackney (1792-7), was another of the few recent London churches and is unlikely to have escaped Pocock's attention. Especially before 1812, when Spiller launched a second phase of construction which included the tower and semi-circular columned

Fig. 7. London, St Marylebone Church (Thomas Hardwick Jnr, 1813-17). (*T.H. Shepherd and J. Elmes,* Metropolitan Improvements, *1827, opp. p. 36.*)

Fig. 8. London, St Martin Outwich, Bishopgate (S.P. Cockerell, 1796-8). (*George Godwin*, The Churches of London, *II, 1839.*)

porches, Hackney's façades – with their sparing use of a conservative Palladian repertoire – sit comfortably alongside several of Pocock's chapel designs.

For the Anglicans, by 1819 there was general agreement about the ideal church plan whatever the style, and followed with only minor modifications in a line that can be traced back to Wren's St James, Piccadilly (1676-84), which its architect saw as the ideal Protestant church: 'beautiful and convenient, and as such, the cheapest of any form I could invent'.[36] James Gibbs used it as the basis for his St Martin-in-the-Fields (1722-6) – conveniently illustrated in his *A Book of Architecture*, 1728[37] – and this was the most widely used layout for the next century, as well as the favoured model for the generation that slotted between Waterloo and the birth of Ecclesiology. The arrangement was uncomplicated, functionally efficient and it was capable of endless modifications. A rectangular body has a portico and tower at one end and a shallow recess for the altar at the other. The western corners are occupied by staircases and those at the east by vestries. However, alternatives were occasionally considered. Jesse Gibson's circular St Peter-Le-Poor, Old Broad Street, London (1788-92),[38] and Spiller's cruciform church in Hackney, discussed above, are notable exceptions. Subsequently, three West Yorkshire churches by Thomas Taylor with short transepts (mid-1820s) and John Shaw's imaginative St Dunstan's-in-the-West, London (1831-3) with an octagonal plan were interesting, but rare Gothic alternatives to the rectangle. The elevations of many of the Classical post-Waterloo churches can also be traced back to St Martin-in-the-Fields, which, like its plan, was usefully transmitted for easy adaptation *via* the pages of Gibbs' *A Book of Architecture* – the eighteenth century's most influential pattern book – and one by no means obsolete a century after publication. The early nineteenth-century architects merely had to change Gibbs' Roman Corinthian order to any of the currently fashionable Greek ones, something their training had qualified all but the most inept to do convincingly.

Gothic presented the real challenge, but also the area of greatest need: how best could the Gibbs plan – a form eminently suited to Georgian liturgy, but quite without medieval precedent – be provided with a suitably medieval dress? A writer in 1823 complained, 'It is notorious that many *modern Churches* … have been built in what is usually termed the *Gothic Style;* and it is equally notorious that most of these Edifices have provoked more censure than praise, and entailed on their Architects the reproachful remarks of the scientific Antiquary and the tasteful Connoisseur.'[39] For Pocock, finding sound examples of 'modern Gothic' was problematic as most of the few recent churches were Classical, especially in London, and the wave of Gothic church building that followed the 1818 Act had yet to materialise. Beazley's Gothic tower at St Mary, Faversham, Kent (1799) – which Pocock would have known – was a scarce exception. For an architect based in the capital, Wren's Gothic work would

Fig. 9. London, St Dunstan's-in-the-East (tower by Christopher Wren, 1670-1; body by David Laing, 1817-21). (*George Godwin*, The Churches of London, *I, 1839.*)

have been a logical place to start, and he might well have studied St Alban's, Wood Street or St Mary Aldermary;[40] interestingly St Dunstan-in-the-East not only had a Wren tower, but the rest of the church was in the process of being rebuilt – by David Laing – as Pocock was writing his book and Laing conveniently published his designs in 1818,[41] a rare example of mid-1810s Gothic in London (**Fig. 9**). The style had been more popular in the provinces where a small number of impressive churches had been erected including a handful in Bath and Bristol that might well have been known in London; John Palmer's All Saints, Bath was opened in 1794 and conveniently illustrated in a print published that year.[42]

The *Plates* of Pocock's book

A more detailed examination of Pocock's plates will repay attention. While the elevations are often engaging, his real strength is in his planning, some of which reveal unusual imagination. For convenience, this writer has grouped the plates by assumed denomination and style, and the analysis begins with the Nonconformist chapels. It is here that he is at his most economical and is especially sparing with his Classical ornament, noticeably in his general avoidance of expensive external columns and even pilasters. He seems to have been especially wedded to semi-circular-topped windows — sometimes set within a blind arch — a feature much exploited by his former master, Hardwick, as well as by Spiller at Hackney.

Plates 1 and 2 are austere, one intended to hold 200 persons and the other to contain 350, priced respectively at £650 and £1500. In both, the rectangular plan places the preacher in the centre of the shorter wall, facing the doors at the opposite end. Architectural embellishment is confined to the entrance front and is of a basic form — that which Pocock refers to as 'elegant simplicity'. The Ranelagh Chapel, Plates 9-12, seems to be the only one of the fourteen designs to have been built. A plain two-storey rectangle, it is fundamentally merely a bigger version of the schemes in Plates 1 and 2. The remaining three designs for chapels are more imaginative. Plates 3-5 also have an economically designed principal front, dominated by the over-scaled giant pilasters at each corner. However, the plan is more engaging: two storeys of semi-circlular seating focusing on the pulpit with the more-or-less triangular spaces left as the curve is slotted into the rectangular shell conveniently filled by gallery staircases. This is an eminently rational arrangement which places the preacher in the centre of the long wall — surrounded by his audience — unlike the much more usual Nonconformist horseshoe plan positioning the preacher at an often excessive distance from the back of the chapel. Plates 17-20 are devoted to a substantial chapel, capable of holding 2,000 worshippers, organised on three levels. The plan is a rectangle with segmental convex curves added to the short sides, Pocock's favoured arrangement. The first gallery continues around the entire space — like that at Claremont Chapel mentioned above — but the upper one runs around only three sides.

The most interesting of the chapel designs is that shown in Plates 13-16. The structure is a two-storey octagon set within a square on the ground floor with the triangular spaces given over to staircases and vestries. Upper level seating is entirely uniform, although the ground floor is something of a compromise with a communion table in the side facing the entrances and the pulpit off-centre. Seating focuses on the pulpit, but without the neatness of that in the gallery. The ceiling, supported by slender (presumably) cast-iron columns, rises into a huge octagonal

Fig. 10. Peter Nicholson, 'Principal Elevation of a Chapel', Plate XXII of his *The New Practical Buidler*, 1823, but reproduced in many of Nicholson's later books. It is a reworking of Pocock's Plate 27 and thus greatly extended the influence of this adaptable composition.

crown, surmounted by a substantial octagonal cupola to light the central space. Had it been constructed, the result might well have been an impressive interior.[43]

Pocock illustrated four Classical churches deemed by the present writer to be for Anglican worship, the first three of which have much in common with the rectangular Nonconformist plans. In these, one might conclude he was keen to demonstrate as many variations on his themes as possible, thus in Plates 21 and 25, the majority of the seats face east, but with the easternmost seats facing north and south to the pulpit, whereas in Plate 32, all the seats face east; in Plates 21 and 32, pulpit and reading desk are placed at either side of the altar – as the Commissioners demanded – but in Plate 25, they are united in a single structure directly in front of the altar. Of the elevations, Plates 22 and 27 incorporate towers in the form of drums and, arguably, lack sufficient scale to impress. However, there is a respectable precedent for this which Pocock would have known – S.P. Cockerell's St Martin Outwich, in the City of London (1796-8). Plate 22 appears to reflect Cockerell's design in other ways too, but the device Pocock uses to support the base of the tower – not unlike a wall-mounted funerary monument – seems to be without precedent in this context. A drum shaped tower was a feature exploited by several post-1819 architects, including Robert Smirke, the Inwoods and Francis Bedford. While they generally used the form more robustly than Pocock, it cannot be denied that he probably encouraged their consideration of this form.

The elevation in Plate 27, with a pair of Doric columns *in antis* has much in common with John Soane's design for the gate lodges of Langley Park, Norfolk, illustrated in his *Plans, Elevations and Sections of Buildings* of 1788,[44] a book Pocock might well have owned. Plate 27 can also be linked to a design subsequently published by Peter Nicholson in 1823.[45] Nicholson was a prolific publisher of pattern books; he was also adept at reusing the plates from his earlier books and thus guaranteed a huge readership for a design largely borrowed from Pocock (**Fig. 10**).

The scheme shown in Plates 32-4 is the one closest to the much copied St Martin-in-the-Fields, but here suitably updated to reflect 1819 Greek fashions. In addition to the Gibbsian plan, Pocock reuses its symmetrically placed doors at either end of the long north and south walls and, like Gibbs, sets them within a pair of *in antis* columns. For the west façade, Pocock specified a portico of four Ionic columns with a panelled pilaster at each end, a motif he also exploited in Plate 5. The plan, shown in Plate 32, reveals an unusually deep chancel – its depth no doubt dictated by the grand entrances and staircase vestibules at the east ends of the north and south elevations – crowned by a Soanian 'starfish' ceiling.

Pocock's final and most remarkable church design is illustrated in Plates 35-6, to accommodate 2,500 at a cost which 'would not be short of £40,000'.[46] The plan,

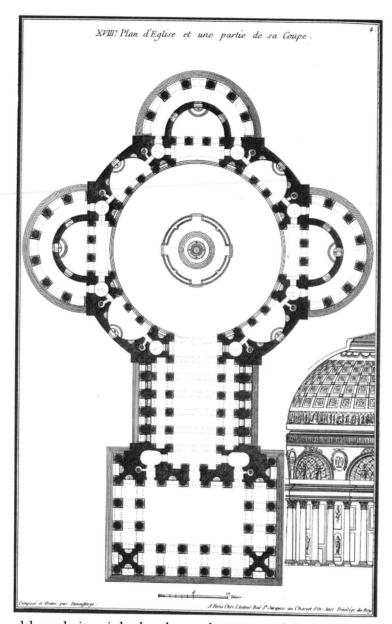

Fig. 11. François de Neuf-forge, plan of a circular church from his *Recueil élémentaire d'architecture*, VII, 1757-68, pl. 4.

although it might be deemed an extended version of George Steuart's St Chad's, Shrewsbury (1790-2), was more likely inspired by a scheme illustrated in François de Neufforge's *Recueil élémentaire d'architecture* (**Fig. 11**).[47] This, surely, was a piece of self-indulgence on Pocock's part: its colossal size made it a superficially memorable design but at the same time precluded execution.

In addition, he offered four Gothic designs. In the post-Waterloo church-building programme, the real challenge fell to those architects whose patrons demanded a Gothic scheme. Pocock's medievalism is a curious confection. It has little in common with the more serious of the early nineteenth-century examples, for instance those of Thomas Rickman or Thomas Taylor, and seems rather closer to the eighteenth-century tradition of Henry Keene, the Adam brothers (**Fig. 12**), John Carr and

James Wyatt, as well as that of Beazley in the tower at Faversham, a job undertaken while Pocock was in his office. Pocock's Gothic has a two-dimensional quality, a piece of background scenery, rather than a solid form. However, his research is likely to have been diligent. Some of the details, for instance the quatrefoils, buttresses and pinnacles, can be found in Batty Langley; Pocock's Plate 24 owes much to Keene's Hartwell Church, Buckinghamshire (1753-5) while the octagonal tower of Plate 31 is likely to be a careless adaptation of Fonthill Abbey in Wiltshire (1796-1812).[48] The unusual panelled buttresses and strong horizontals of Plate 29 were possibly influenced by Hawksmoor's west front of Westminster Abbey (designed 1734), an obvious source for a London architect. All four designs use simple 'Y' tracery in the windows, a form with some medieval precedents, but in the early nineteenth century, one to be found extensively where medieval tracery had decayed and been replaced in post-Reformation repairs.

Given Pocock's willingness to experiment with alternatives to the parallelogram in his Classical proposals, it seems somewhat strange that he didn't consider a Gothic scheme with transepts, a type that several slightly earlier architects had exploited.[49] A cruciform plan was also used by Spiller at Hackney (1792-7) – discussed above – which, although Classical, was an important 'new' church for Pocock's era.[50]

Fig. 12. Edinburgh, St George's Chapel, York Place (Robert and James Adam, 1794). (*T. H. Shepherd and J. Britton,* Modern Athens … or Edinburgh in the Nineteenth Century, *1831, opp. p. 42.*)

Fig. 13. Liverpool, Wesleyan Chapel, Stanhope Street (opened 1827). (Lancashire Illustrated, *1831, opp. p. 73.*)

Of the six designs for Classical towers, four are essentially Grecian re-workings of Gibbs's published designs, and two have curious pierced Grecian spires. The altarpieces largely revert to eighteenth-century types and the final pulpit scheme has much in common with Spiller's at Hackney.[51]

The book's influence

How useful was Pocock's *Designs for Churches and Chapels*? Certainly it *ought* to have been eagerly seized by those intent on building and by the architects they employed; after all there were no published alternatives until 1836 and new churches and chapels were built in large numbers in the 1820s. Perhaps the answer lies in two supplementary questions: how well had he identified the architectural fashions of the post-Waterloo period, and as an architect, how good was he at responding to them? Once again it is helpful to divide the designs into three groups.

As a designer of Nonconformist chapels, Pocock was probably at his most influential. The book offers models from large to small and he successfully exploits a modest, pared down, often astylar Classicism to their embellishment. A large number, erected in the 1820s and 1830s reveal façades composed of elements from his designs. A handful of examples will suffice: Trinity Chapel, Brixton, London (1828);[52] Brunswick Chapel, Macclesfield, Cheshire (1823);[53] Mount Zion Chapel, Sheffield (1834)[54] and the Wesleyan Chapel, Stanhope Street, Liverpool (1827) (**Fig. 13**), an adaptation of Pocock's Plates 2 and 12. Most obviously, Plate 27 enjoyed extensive popularity. It was the inspiration for the Oddfellows' Hall, Barnsley (W.J. Hindle, 1836); the Wesleyan Chapel in Bridport, Dorset (perhaps by Joseph Galpin, 1838) (**Fig. 14**);[55] the Strict Baptist Chapel, Shaw Street, Liverpool (1847);[56] and as late as 1849, it was still considered to be a viable model for the Primitive Methodist Chapel, Great Thornton Street, Hull (William Sissons).

Perhaps most imaginatively, Pocock's willingness to use shapes other than the standard rectangle provides a number of functional alternatives for pulpit-led patterns of worship. Of course, he was not the first to exploit these shapes and so claims for the book's influence in this respect can only be tentative. Nevertheless, a number of 1820s and 1830s chapels probably owe their form to him, notably the octagonal Mount Zion Chapel in Birmingham (1823)[57] and the semi-circular Old Chapel, Willingham, Cambridgeshire (1830).[58]

Fig. 14. Bridport, Dorset, former Wesleyan Chapel (attributed to Joseph Galpin, 1838). (*Timothy Connor.*)

Fig. 15. London, St John, Waterloo Rd (Francis Bedford, 1823-4). (*T.H. Shepherd and J. Elmes,* Metropolitan Improvements, *1827, after p. 162.*)

So far as the Church of England was concerned, Pocock arguably misread the intentions of those intending to build with the assistance of the Church Building Commission and none of his designs came anywhere near the popularity of Gibbs's St Martin-in-the-Fields a century earlier. The Commissioners generally wanted big churches, and ones generously embellished with ornament, at least on the street front. For the Classical ones, a handsome portico became *de rigueur* and for the Gothic ones, something that suggested that the churches were worthy successors to the medieval tradition – without, of course, straying too far towards 'Popery' – was required. On both counts, Pocock was wide of the mark. Rickman's Holy Trinity, Bristol (**Fig. 2**), Goodwin's St George, Hulme, Manchester (**Fig. 3**) and Francis Bedford's St John, Waterloo Road, London (**Fig. 15**), all well-regarded churches and recipients of the Commissioners' largesse, are somewhat at odds with those in Pocock's book. Nevertheless, his influence can be found in several privately funded

Classical Anglican churches, including: St George, Brighton (Charles Busby, 1824); St John, Cheltenham (J.B. Papworth, 1827-9); and St Swithun, Allington, Dorset (Charles Wallace, 1826-7).

Of the better Gothic church designers in the 1820s – for instance, R.D. Chantrell, Thomas Rickman, Thomas Taylor and Lewis Vulliamy – their success owed little to Pocock. However, for a lower level of the profession, the book was of real value. St Peter, Frimley, Surrey (1825) and the new front to St Mary Magdalene, Bermondsey, London (1830), by J. T. Parkinson and George Porter respectively, both minor architect/ surveyors, owe much to the Pocock's philosophy of applying Gothic details to a flat surface. The most obvious adaptation of a Pocock design is the Octagon Chapel, Wisbech, Cambridgeshire (1826-30) – based clearly on Plate 8 – designed by a local builder/engineer, William Swansborough (**Fig. 16**). And three alternative designs by Charles Busby for St Andrew and St Mary Magdalene, Maidenhead, Berkshire (1822)[59] owe much to Plate 24. However, it is worth noting that the thin Gothic detailing of Pocock's designs – lacking medieval precedent probably intentionally rather than through laziness or ignorance – found a resonance with Nonconformists as Gothic gradually came to be seen by them as an acceptable alternative to 'the modern style'. The Wesleyan Chapel, Acorn Street, Sheffield (*c*.1823) (**Fig. 17**) and Congregational Chapel, Halesworth, Suffolk (1836),[60] while not direct copies of

Fig. 16. Wisbech, Cambridge-shire, Octagonal Chapel (William Swansborough, 1826-30), nineteenth-century photograph by Samuel Smith. (*Wisbech and Fenland Museum.*)

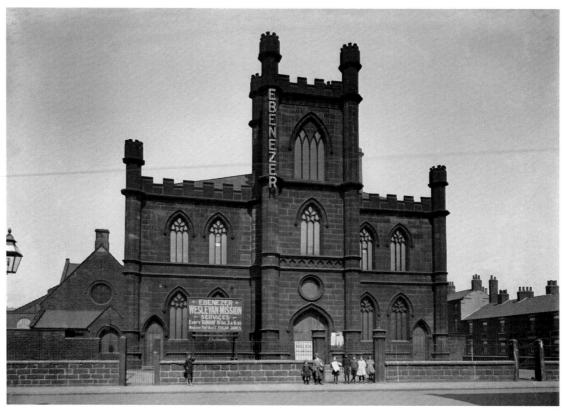

Fig. 17. Sheffield, Wesleyan Chapel, Acorn Street (Joseph Botham, c.1823). (*Reproduced by permission of English Heritage, NMR*)

any of Pocock's designs, nevertheless share his approach to the style.[61] Although it is true that the book was the only one devoted to the design of churches and chapels before Hamilton's inept 1836 offering, architects seeking inspiration were not entirely abandoned by publishers. John Britton and Augustus Pugin's *Illustrations of the Public Buildings of London* (first edition 1825-8), included a number of plates of recently built Classical churches, which, although small in scale, neatly set out the buildings in plans, elevations and sections, the ideal medium from which an architect could borrow. And for those intent on designing a Gothic edifice, books like Pugin's *Specimens of Gothic Architecture* (1821-3) and Britton's *Cathedral Antiquities of England* series (1814–35), while not containing designs for complete new churches, at least included painstakingly measured and delineated details capable of adaptation, and arguably had a greater influence on the course of the Gothic Revival than Pocock's offerings.

The first edition of his *Designs* in 1819 was a commendably far-sighted initiative, anticipating substantial demand for the book; by the date of the second edition, in 1823, the first wave of Commissioners' churches were being constructed and many more were in prospect. However, it is hard to imagine there would be serious interest in a third edition in 1835, except from his faithful Nonconformist clientele. Pocock had failed to predict the sort of churches that would be required in the 1820s and a decade later his designs were largely unfashionable, especially the Gothic ones. A review in the *British Critic* in 1840 was merciless. 'What can be more promising than such a title? … yet a book of such shameless vulgarity we never did set our eyes upon. Here is the whole art and mystery of building churches as much like meeting houses as ever we possibly can … a friend has sent the volume to us as a rich source of cockneyism; and as such, to those who can afford to collect curiosities, it is worth the money … '[62] And so it goes on.

Given the *British Critic's* reviewer's likely 'High' Anglican standpoint – other articles in 1830s and '40s editions give a clear indication of the journal's intended market – his criticism in 1840 was entirely predictable and might have represented the final nail in Pocock's coffin. However, there is one more chapter to his influence, and a very important one, too: the impact of the book in North America.

Pocock's influence in America

Despite a range of post-1820 indigenous architectural talent and a number of pattern books from American publishers – most notably seven produced by Asher Benjamin[63] – the country continued to look to its former colonial master for stylistic guidance. 'To keep abreast of designs from London, New Yorkers consulted English books. For information … [about] façade treatments, they found models in books by [Peter] Nicholson and William Pocock,'[64] the most widely read of the English post-Waterloo manuals.[65] Pocock's overseas importance should not surprise us; his concept of both Classical and Gothic churches, while lacking sufficient gravitas for earnest English Anglicans, accorded perfectly with a less doctrinaire attitude to architectural style across the Atlantic, as well as to less rigid religious practices there. And as the American Greek Revival lasted at least a generation longer than its English counterpart, Pocock's Classical designs continued to be fashionable long after the style had been dismissed as inappropriate for an English church. Among the Gothic examples, Holy Trinity Lutheran Church, West 21st Street, New York (1868), shares much with Pocock's approach to the style. And Alexander Jackson Davis's unexecuted octagonal design for the Church of the Holy Apostles, New York (1845), takes elements from Pocock's Plates 6 and 13. However, Plate 27 exercised the greatest influence. Its façade arrangement of a pair of Doric columns *in antis*, flanked by pairs of more narrowly spaced pilasters, and crowned by a pediment – with or without a tower – is a type found extensively in the second quarter of the century throughout the eastern seaboard. Significantly, among those who used it are some of America's most eminent architects: South Congregational Church, Middletown, Connecticut (1829), by Davis; St James R.C. Church, James Street, New York

Fig. 18. Baltimore, St Andrew (c.1840), from a nineteenth-century photograph. (*Maryland Historical Society*.)

Pl. LIX.

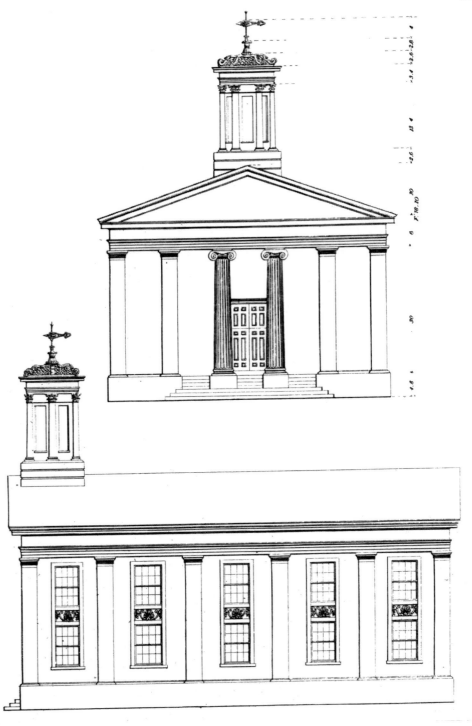

Fig. 19. Asher Benjamin, 'Elevations of a Church', Plate LIX of his *The Architect or Complete Builder's Guide*, 1845 (first edition, 1839), one of the most widely read American pattern books. The related plan – Plate LVIII – is taken from Pocock's Plate 25.

(1835-7), by Minard Lafever; Christ Church (Episcopal), Mobile, Alabama (1838-9), by James Dakin and – somewhat modified – St Mary, Nashville, Tennessee (1845-7), by William Strickland. It was also used by countless less renowned designers, for instance, for Spring Street Presbyterian Church, New York (1835-6), and St Andrew's Church, Baltimore (*c*.1840) (**Fig. 18**).

The influence of Pocock's Plate 27 was considerably extended *via* its appearance in one of Asher Benjamin's pattern books. His early published designs for churches are very much in the 'Colonial' style and for his 1806 *The American Builder's Companion*, of its two churches, one has a hexastyle portico while the other is plain; both have prominent towers and the details of both plates can unmistakably be traced to Gibbs. However, for his *The Architect or Complete Builder's Guide* (first edition 1839, with five subsequent editions over the next twenty-three years), there is a dramatic stylistic shift: conservative Gibbsian Baroque is replaced with up-to-date Greek Revival

Fig. 20. New York, New York (Bowery) Theatre (Ithiel Town, 1828), watercolour by Alexander Jackson Davies. (*Metropolitan Museum of Art, New York*.)

and its single church is a sophisticated proposal. In seeking to explain this change, an obvious explanation is Pocock's *Designs*; Benjamin's 1839 church is yet another version of Pocock's Plate 27 – adapted principally by moving closer together the central columns to regularise the inter-columnation (**Fig. 19**). According to Benjamin 'The expression produced by the simple massive forms composing these elevations will be in accordance with those devotional feelings which naturally arise, in a building devoted to the worship of the Supreme Being.'[66] The author's prose, very much in the late eighteenth-century French Enlightenment tradition, usefully illuminates the gulf between English and American attitudes to religion at this time – this was written, let us not forget, in 1839, the year the Cambridge Camden Society was formed – but this American tradition was one in which Pocock's philosophy of church architecture sat comfortably. This design even had a secular life, perfectly suited to smaller-scale public buildings, for instance the Elizabeth Street façade of the New York (Bowery) Theatre (Ithiel Town, 1828) (**Fig. 20**), and the Old California Capitol, Benicia (1853). Derivatives of Plate 27 can also be found in Canada, for instance Zion Congregational Church, Toronto (William Thomas, 1839-40) and the Garrison Chapel, Halifax, Nova Scotia (Colonel Calder, 1844-6).

Could Pocock have anticipated his North American success or even intentionally aimed his book at that market? Probably not, but with its first edition appearing at a time when Gibbs's *A Book of Architecture* remained the only widely read manual to include practical church designs, its influence could have been predicted. For the newly empowered American nation, a nation with considerable wealth to devote to public buildings for its rapidly increasing population, and a desire to enhance national prestige through its architectural landmarks, a publication with a range of modern church designs, catering for all sizes and stylistic alternatives, was ideally placed to capture this huge market.

oooooOooooo

Since this Introduction was prepared for publication, a remarkable piece of information has emerged: could Pocock's book have had an influence on a project by Karl Freidrich Schinkel, arguably the most inventive early-nineteenth-century German architect? His rebuilding of the façade of Berlin Cathedral (1819-22, demolished *c.*1894) bears a notable resemblance to Plate 27, even including Pocock's idiosyncratic 'pepper-pot' towers.

The writer is deeply indebted to Terry Friedman for numerous helpful suggestions in the preparation of this essay. Thanks are also due to Colin Dews, Hugh Pagan, Christopher Wakeling and others mentioned in the notes below.

Notes

1. Archives of the Incorporated Church Building Society, Lambeth Palace Library, file 0456.

2. Archives of the Church Building Commission, Church of England Records Centre, file 20573.

3. Francis Bedford was deemed by the *Gentleman's Magazine's* critic (Nov. 1825, pp.392-5) to have committed a number of solecisms in his design for Holy Trinity, Newington Butts, London (1823-4). The critic objected to the Doric order in the tower being placed above the Corinthian order of the portico, as well as the decoration around the altar: 'Architects should know that a distinction ought to be made between the altar of a Church and the upper end of a Presbyterian Conventicle.' (p. 394).

4. For the Society, see C. Webster and J. Elliott (eds) *'A Church as it should be': the Cambridge Camden Society and its Influence*, Shaun Tyas, 2000.

5. Mention should also be made of: W.C. Wilson, *Helps to the Building of Churches, Parsonage Houses, and Schools*, Foster, 1835, although it contained only one church design, despite its title.

6. C. Campbell, *Vitruvius Britannicus*, for the author, vol. 1, 1715, p. 1.

7. R. and J. Adam, *Works in Architecture*, for the authors, vol. 1., 1778, p. 4.

8. J. Paine, *Plans, Elevations and Sections of Noblemen's ... Houses*, for the author, 1767, p. ii.

9. M.H. Port, *Six Hundred New Churches: the Church Building Commission, 1818-1856*, Spire Books, 2006, p. 7.

10. Parliamentary Papers 1837-8, (325) XXXVIII, pp.141 *et seq.*

11. I am very grateful to Michael Port for this information. See also Port [note 9], p. 276. These figures do not include the 186 alterations and extensions to existing churches carried out in this period and included in the Drawback Account. To extend the figures for new churches to the full quarter-century of this essay is problematical. Very few new churches would have been completed between 1815 and 1817 – the first one in the statistics above is St Pancras Church – but many more were built between 1838 and 1840. A writer in the *Church Builder*, 1, 1862, pp. 40-3, claims an average of 100 new churches per year were built between 1830 and 1850, although he offers no basis for the calculation and the figures appear very high on the basis of those accurate ones in the Drawback Account.

12. W.F. Pocock, *Designs for Churches and Chapels*, J. Taylor, 1819, pp. 6 and 13.

13. C. Binfield, 'Architects in Connexion: Four Methodist Generations', in J. Garnet and C. Matthew (eds), *Revival and Religion since 1700*, Hambleton Press, 1993, pp. 153-81.

14. H. Colvin, *A Biographical Dictionary of British Architects, 1600-1840*, Yale, 2008, pp. 818-19. Much of Colvin's account is based on an unpublished 'Memoir' by W.W. Pocock, W.F. Pocock's son, in the RIBA Library.

15. This is an on-line dictionary, to be found on the Wesley Historical Society's website. www. wesleyhistoricalsociety.org.uk

16. Binfield [note 13], p. 158.

17. Colvin [note 14], p. 818.

18. Pocock [note 12], p. 13.

19. Although he designed a number in the 1820s and 1830s. See Binfield [note 13], p. 160.

20. All the editions were published by the Taylors, most of them are by Josiah. Pocock also published the technical manual *Observations on Bond in Brickwork* in 1839.

21. Pocock [note 12], p. 13.

22. Ibid., p. 7.

23. Ibid.

24. Ibid., p. 9.
25. 'Letter to a Friend on the Commission for Building Fifty New Churches', quoted in Lydia M. Soo, *Wren's "Tracts" on Architecture and Other Writings*, Cambridge U.P., 1998, p. 115.
26. Published by Longman *et al.*, 1812. Plate 7 shows 'The Theatre of Herodes Atticus at Athens'.
27. Pocock [note 12], p. 10.
28. Ibid., p. 11.
29. Binfield [note 13], p. 155.
30. Colvin [note 14], p. 573.
31. See T. Friedman, 'The Octagon Chapel, Norwich', in *The Georgian Group Journal*, 13, 2003, pp. 54-77.
32. Designed by John Walmsley. Illustrated in *Lancashire Illustrated*, Fisher, Son and Jackson, 1831, p. 73.
33. D. Stillman, *English Neo-Classical Architecture*, Zwemmer, II, 1988, p. 442.
34. Quoted in Stillman [note 33], p. 446.
35. J. Summerson, *Georgian London*, Yale, 2003, p. 245.
36. S. Wren, *Parentalia*, 1750, p. 320, quoted in Soo [note 25], p. 115.
37. J. Gibbs, *A Book of Architecture*, for the author, 1728, pls 1-7.
38. See T. Friedman, 'The Church of St Peter-le-Poor Reconsidered', *Architectural History*, 43, 2000, pp. 162-71.
39. This appears in the 'Address' – essentially a prospectus – for A. Pugin, *Specimens of Gothic Architecture*, J. Taylor, 1823, in one of Taylor's catalogues.
40. The building history of St Mary is complicated and the tower was by William Dickinson, Wren's one time assistant, rather than by Wren himself. However, for Pocock's generation, this would have been seen as a 'Wren' church.
41. D. Laing, *Plans etc of Buildings Public and Private,* Taylor, 1818.
42. From a drawing by William Watts.
43. The idea of an octagon within a square had earlier been exploited by Thomas Lightoler for the Octagon Chapel, Bath (opened 1767), the drawings for which were subsequently published. However, Pocock's arrangement is a significantly more rational version of the possibilities the shape offers.
44. Published by Messrs Taylor, 1788, plate 23.
45. P. Nicholson, *New Practical Builder*, Thomas Kelly, 1823, pl. XXIII.
46. Pocock [note 12], p. 26.
47. The Parisian publication ran to 8 volumes, 1757-68. Circular churches appear in vol. VII, pls 4-5.
48. Pocock certainly knew Fonthill well enough to take a potential client to visit it in 1823. Binfield [note 13], p. 163.
49. For examples, see Nigel Yates, *Buildings, Faith and Worship*, Oxford, 1991, chapter 5.
50. D. Mander, *St John-at-Hackney*, The Parish of Hackney, *c*.2000.
51. Spiller's drawings are in Sir John Soane's Museum, 47/8/17-18.
52. Illustrated in C. Stell, *Nonconformist Chapels and Meeting Houses in Eastern England*, English Heritage, 2002, p. 105.
53. Illustrated in C. Stell, *Nonconformist Chapels and Meeting Houses in Northern England*, HMSO, 1994, p. 21.
54. Illustrated in Stell, *Northern* [note 53], p. 308.
55. T. Connor, 'Too Late for the *Dictionary*? Joseph Galpin and late-Georgian Architecture in West Dorset', in *Georgian Group Journal*, XVII, 2009, pp. 141-54. I am grateful to Mr Connor for

additional information on this subject.

56. Illustrated in Stell, *Northern* [note 53], p. 104.

57. Illustrated in B. Little, *Birmingham Buildings*, David and Charles, 1971, plate 43.

58. Illustrated in Stell, *Eastern* [note 52], pp. 44-5.

59. Illustrated in N. Bingham, *C.A. Busby Regency Architect of Brighton and Hove*, RIBA, 1991, pp. 60-1.

60. Illustrated in Stell, *Eastern* [note 52], p. 290.

61. Of Pocock's 1837 Christ Church, Virginia Water, Surrey, 'no attempt at accurate detail' is not unreasonable. I. Nairn and N. Pevsner, *The Buildings of England: Surrey*, Penguin, 1982, p. 493.

62. *British Critic and Quarterly Theological Review*, 28, 1840, p. 471.

63. T. Hamlin, *Greek Revival Architecture in America,* Dover, 1964, pp. 163-4.

64. Morrison Heckscher, 'Building the Empire City: Architects and Architecture', in *Art and the Empire City: New York, 1825-1861*, Metropolitan Museum of Art and Yale UP, 2000, p. 171. I am most grateful to Mr Heckscher for additional information on this topic. Hamlin [note 63] states that several of the designs in Chester Hill, *The Builder's Guide*, Appleton, New York, 1836, 'are taken line for line from Peter Nicholson' (pp. 165-6.) For more on Nicholson's American influence, see Hamlin [note 63], p. 210; 339-42

65. For assistance with Pocock's New York influence, I am grateful to Mariam Touba and Sue Kriete of the New York Historical Society's library.

66. 3rd edition, 1845, p. 49.

DESIGNS

FOR

CHURCHES AND CHAPELS

OF

VARIOUS DIMENSIONS AND STYLES, &c.

LONDON:
PRINTED BY JAMES MOYES,
Castle Street, Leicester Square.

DESIGNS

FOR

CHURCHES AND CHAPELS

OF

VARIOUS DIMENSIONS AND STYLES;

CONSISTING OF

PLANS, ELEVATIONS, AND SECTIONS:

With Estimates.

ALSO

SOME DESIGNS

FOR

ALTARS, PULPITS, AND STEEPLES.

By W. F. POCOCK, ARCHITECT.

Third Edition.

LONDON:

PRINTED FOR M. TAYLOR,

NEPHEW AND SUCCESSOR TO THE LATE JOSIAH TAYLOR,

6 BARNARD'S INN, HOLBORN.

1835.

PREFACE.

It is a fact generally acknowledged, that there is not, at the present period, in this Country, sufficient accommodation for the inhabitants in the Buildings erected for Religious Worship: a circumstance which demands the most serious attention, if we consider the nature and importance of religion, and the effects a proper observance of its public ordinances produces on the morals and happiness of the people. The disproportion between the population, and the number of persons that the places of public worship will contain, varies in almost every parish; but in no part of the kingdom, perhaps, is this inconvenience so sensibly felt, as in the environs of the Metropolis, which may be caused by the great extent of some of the parishes, and the extraordinary increase of the population within them during the last twenty years.

No small degree of credit is due to the Government of the country, that, while they have seen this deficiency, they have, at

the same time, endeavoured to remedy it, by liberal grants of
money towards the erection of new " Churches," or " Chapels,"
where they are wanted, or of repairing the old. And this has
been aided by subscriptions, for the same purpose, that are truly
characteristic of the liberality and piety of the British nation.

It is not intended, however, entirely to relieve the various
parishes from the expense of providing places of public worship ;
but rather to afford that assistance, without which, new Churches
would not be begun ; or, if begun, could not be completed, on
account of the great additional burden that would fall on the
parishioners. These circumstances have led to the present
publication, which it is hoped will assist the views of Ministers
and others who are desirous of promoting the best interests of
the people.

It has always been considered advisable, for the proposers
of any measure of a public nature to be prepared with some
specific outline of a plan, that will be best calculated to answer
the intended purpose, and least likely to meet with opposition.
There are two points to which the attention should be principally directed in the building of Churches—the *number it is
necessary to accommodate, and the expense that will probably attend
it.* I have, therefore, in the description of these Designs, given
the number each will contain, and an estimate of the expense,
in order that the question may be brought into a small compass.

I have purposely avoided every thing that is splendid and magnificent; and have studied to produce such Designs only, as are plain, suitable to the purpose, and at the least possible expense.

A writer on Architecture says, that " every building should, " by its appearance, express its destination and purpose, and " that some *character* should prevail therein, which is suitable " to, and expressive of, the peculiar end it has to answer. To " effect this will require the exertion of the powers of the " mind, the fire of genius, and solidity of judgment; and with- " out this, a composition is but a compilation of parts without " meaning or end." Without pretending to the high qualities here mentioned, I have attempted a simplicity of style, not only from taste, but as it happily accords with economy; yet I have been attentive to elegance, by avoiding every thing that is mean or vulgar in appearance. Those who are acquainted with the Art of Design know, that it is much more pleas- ing to the artist, by boldness of outline, and richness in decoration, to form compositions which produce a striking effect, than to have his powers cramped by the chilling in- fluence of a rigid economy: but the great expense of building in the present day, renders it necessary that this should be one of the first considerations, and that what is deficient in grandeur should be made up by elegant simplicity.

A considerable difference of opinion has prevailed respecting the form of buildings best calculated for religious worship. The old heathen temples will not assist our ideas on the subject, as they were not intended to contain the worshippers in public assemblies. They sacrificed individually, or in small parties; only the principal personages attended the altar, the multitude remained without. In the celebration of their rites, seldom more than a small portion of the people attended at the temple at the same time: it is materially different with us, who are enjoined to attend the worship of God on the same day. In the temple built by Solomon, at Jerusalem, the altar for the sacrifice of the burnt-offering was without the building, in front of the portico; only the altar for the offering of incense was within the house, where the priests officiated alone. The Santa Sophia, built by Constantine, in the city bearing his name, was in the form of a cross, the well-known symbol used by that Emperor, with a dome of a peculiar construction, rising from the intersection of the nave and transept. The long-drawn aisles this form affords, as exemplified also in our ancient cathedrals, are well adapted to the lengthened processions of the Greek and Roman churches; but they are not so well calculated for the simplicity and purity of Protestant worship. The Roman Catholic churches on the Continent are mostly without pews, or fixed seats, throughout the principal part of the building; they are generally confined to that part which we call the choir, while the major part of the congregation have moveable chairs, which are placed according to the fancy of the individuals who occupy them: I have remarked some churches, however, which had fixed seats and pews immediately round the pulpit.

In the Protestant or Reformed Churches, the principal point for consideration is, *the most convenient method of seating the greatest number of persons to hear distinctly the voice of the reader and preacher.* The only buildings of antiquity constructed for the purpose of holding an audience were the theatres; these are, consequently, the only authorities applicable to the case to which we can refer. Both the Greek and Roman theatres were formed nearly upon the same principles; they differed chiefly in the ichnography. Of these, the Grecian is to be preferred for our purpose; it is not so simple as the Roman, but it will contain more spectators in the same space. To explain this, it may be observed, that the seats of the spectators (denominated *cunei*, or *wedges*, from the *wedge-like* form of their divisions by the avenues which radiated from the centre), in both cases, rose from the ground behind each other in regular gradation; in the Roman theatres they formed a *semicircle* in front of the proscenium, and enclosed the orchestra; while in the Greek edifices this formed a greater portion of the circle, like the round part of the Greek letter omega (Ω), or as we commonly say, a horse-shoe; it consequently enclosed more space, and gave a longer line for the seats, with the same advantages to the spectators. In buildings of dimensions so large, that the voice of the speaker can hardly reach the extent of the semicircular, or Roman form, it would not be advisable to sweep it off to a greater distance, like the Grecian; but in those of moderate size, where the whole of the auditors are within the compass of his voice, no objection on that account can be made to the adoption of the latter; for it will be found on experiment, that some persons placed at a distance in front of the speaker hear as distinctly as others placed considerably nearer on his side; consequently, this form may be adopted with propriety in buildings of much greater magnitude. In addition to this, the ideas and feelings of gentlemen in the habit of public speaking may be adduced, who unanimously agree in preferring, when they address a large audience, the major part of them being placed in front; and I have, also, been informed that they can soon ascertain whether their voice is distinctly heard. I have, therefore, chiefly proposed the figure of a parallelogram, with a portion of a circle at the extremity, which comes nearest to the form here recommended.

It will be observed, that the modern practice in constructing buildings for holding an audience is to cover more than once the site of the edifice. The floor is first appropriated for seats; when more are required, they are obtained by raising galleries against the walls; these nearly approach the form of the seats in the ancient theatres: the galleries (or porticos, as Vitruvius calls them) in those buildings were appropriated for the seats of the women; but as they were without roofs or other covering, except temporary awnings to shade the audience from the heat of the sun, their construction was, of course, materially different. It will be seen, that our modern edifices of religious worship are formed by combining the spectatory part of the ancient buildings before alluded to with the cells of their temples. Both these possessing the utmost simplicity in their respective forms, have been carried into all the various figures that the imaginations of the moderns could devise; but it is to be hoped that good sense, sound judgment, and correct taste, are now so generally diffused, that public opinion will check this exuberance, and introduce a more chaste and correct style. The construction of more than one gallery has by some been objected to, but I think without any solid reason: it is a very good expedient to contain a large audience in a building so small as to allow of the preacher's voice being heard in every part. It must be admitted, that it partakes rather too much of the appearance of our theatres, which are constructed in such a manner for this purpose; but I do not see that we are obliged to give up the convenience on that account; for a building may be designed with this accommodation, and still possess all the solemnity proper to a place set apart for religious worship.

It is now necessary to mention a circumstance which, to
general readers, may prove dry and uninteresting, but which is
known to every one actually engaged in business to be a subject
of the first consideration; and I trust I shall be excused for
entering into a minute detail. The proper method to be pur-
sued in order to get the work executed in the best manner, and
on the most reasonable terms, is by contract and competition
among respectable tradesmen, under the direction of an able and
experienced Architect; by which means the amount of the
expense may be accurately ascertained before the work is begun.
It is to be supposed that several meetings, or consultations, will
be held before any definite plan can be determined on; but it
being agreed that a building shall be erected to contain *a certain
number of persons*, either at a sum specified, or at an expense
which is afterwards to be arranged, it will be found necessary to
direct some Architect to make designs agreeably to this inten-
tion, with an estimate of the probable expense. After these
have been approved, proper working drawings must be prepared,
with specifications of all the artificers' works in detail : these
should be laid before a committee appointed at the last meeting ;
which being approved, a list should be formed of a certain number of tradesmen of respectable character, and possessing means
equal to the magnitude of the work. These persons should
then be invited to deliver in a proposal, stating for what sum
they would undertake to execute the whole of the work, agreeably to the designs and specifications prepared for the purpose ;

and they should, also, be requested to attend with their proposals at a certain time. The committee being assembled, and all the parties in attendance, the tenders are to be opened, and the sums written in a list against the respective names. The name against the lowest sum is then to be minuted, and the list of the *sums only* exhibited to the parties; by which means all the offers are known, but the names being concealed, no unpleasant sensation is felt; each person being able only to recognise his own. This method I can recommend from experience; having found that it has given great satisfaction, and prevented all private intelligence and undue influence.

It may be necessary to observe, in conclusion, that this work has not been undertaken without consideration; the circumstances in which I have been placed for many years past, having led me to study Ecclesiastical Architecture, which is not quite in the general line of practice; and I may, therefore, without vanity, hope that I am not entirely destitute of that information which is necessary for constructing buildings of this description. Some of the Designs have been long made for particular situations, and one I have lately carried into execution in the parish of Chelsea. I feel so well assured of the attention with which they have been considered by myself, that I trust they will bear strict examination by others, and that they will fully answer the purpose intended, particularly in those essential points, *the accommodation of the greatest number of persons, at the least possible expense;* at the same time keeping in view that substantiality of construction and propriety of appearance which they require.

It will be a source of great satisfaction, if the work should prove useful to those persons who are engaged in promoting the erection of Edifices for Public Worship, and if, in consulting it, they shall derive any information that may facilitate their labours.

W. F. P.

Knightsbridge.

DESCRIPTION OF THE PLATES.

BEFORE I enter into the Description of the Plates, it is necessary to premise, that the popular opinion of the number of persons in any assembly, is generally incorrect and much exaggerated. In many instances it has been found, on examination, that it did not contain one half the number estimated. This applies also to a congregation assembled in a place of worship; which I particularly request those persons to bear in mind who compare the numbers these Designs are calculated to accommodate, with what it is said other places already erected will contain. The numbers given suppose the congregation to be comfortably seated, but perhaps with those who stand in the aisles, or are otherwise put in on particular occasions, they may be nearly doubled.

It is necessary to remark, that the Estimates are formed on the basis of London prices, for materials and workmanship of the best description: their amounts may be easily diminished or increased, according to local circumstances, either by a percentage, or otherwise, so as to meet the variations of price in different parts of the country. They suppose the greatest economy to be used, and the strictest attention paid to the expenditure, throughout the whole progress of the building; as I am well assured that, unless this scrupulous regard to economy be continued until the final completion of every work, although it was begun upon the most economical plan, yet it will in the conclusion exceed the bounds prescribed.

PLATE I.

PLAN and Elevation of a small Chapel, size 40 feet by 27 feet outside the walls, exclusive of the Vestry, which is intended to have sashes, with doors under, into the Chapel, in order that persons may sit in the room and hear the service. It is calculated to seat 200 persons, and the Vestry 25 more.

Estimate 650*l.*

PLATE II.

Plan and Elevation of a Chapel, with a Porch or covering in front, a School-room and Vestry behind. The Chapel is 40 feet by 36 feet. The School-room 26 feet by 12 feet, which is planned to be used in aid of the Chapel, when occasion may require. The Chapel is calculated to seat 350 persons, and 50 or more children in the School-room.

Estimate 1500*l.*

PLATES III. IV. V.

Ground Plan, Gallery Plan, and Elevation of a Design for a Chapel, or Meeting-house, size 63 feet by 43 feet. This

c

Plan is designed for a Baptists' congregation: a tank for water, connected with suitable attiring rooms is provided.—The steps in the Plan behind the tank lead to the pulpit. The distribution of this Plan is, I think, well adapted for hearing, and will seat 675 persons.

Estimate 3000*l.*

PLATES VI. VII. VIII.

Ground Plan, Gallery Plan, and Elevation for a Chapel in the Gothic style, size 78 feet by 50 feet; will seat 950 persons. A handsome staircase in the vestibule leads to the Galleries, while the side entrances lead into the body of the Chapel. A second Gallery on each side of the organ will afford accommodation for Charity-children, &c. The Vestry is connected with the body of the Chapel by an enclosed passage. The Estimate is 5000*l.*

PLATES IX. X. XI. XII.

Three Plans and Elevation of Ranelagh Chapel, built under my direction, in George Street, near Sloane Square, size 66 feet by 44 feet, and 30 feet high inside. It contains in the basement two School-rooms, one for boys, the other for girls, capable of accommodating 500 children; also the living rooms for the mistress. The line round the buildings shews the extent of the ground. The exact number of sittings in this Chapel I am ignorant of: it is calculated for 900 persons. The free seats are on each side, and extend to the second window. After this Plate was engraved, the pews were altered.

The Plan of the Gallery, Plate XI. shews the situation of the Organ behind the Pulpit; it was originally intended to place the children on each side of the organ, with a staircase from each School-room to their proper Gallery: this arrangement was altered, and there is only one staircase at this end of the Chapel; the space which the other would have occupied is appropriated on the Basement floor to a Sleeping-room for the mistress; and on the Ground Floor to a Robing-room. It is in contemplation to place the children in the back seats of the Gallery, which will accommodate a greater number than where they now sit, and where they will be more out of observation.

Plate XII. shews the Front Elevation. The building is of brick, with stone strings round. The front is finished with stucco, in imitation of stone. The Portico is stone. The roof is of the most simple construction, and is covered with slates, having a gable at the back to answer to the pediment in front, with a ridge between, and eaves on each side: the water does not drop from the eaves, but is received into square troughs well framed together, and supported by Portland stone bearers laid into the walls, giving the appearance of a block cornice, from whence it is brought down in a stack of iron pipes on each side.

The amount of the whole of the bills was 4090*l.* of which near 600*l.* may be assigned to the extra substructure, and fitting up of the School-room, leaving the cost of the Chapel 3500*l.*

PLATES XIII. XIV. XV. XVI.

Ground Plan, Gallery Plan, Section, and Elevation of a Design for an octagon Chapel, 60 feet diameter, with a lantern light in the centre, having seats for 1000 persons, of which 300 are free.   Estimate 4000*l.*

The Plan of the Gallery, Plate XIV. shews that the construction is the same all round; the access is by the staircases in the angles of the square, so as just to get headway under the windows, with the additional rise in the body of the building.

Section through the building, Plate XV. which shews that the roof is very different from what is usually put on buildings of this form : it is both lighter and lower ; the ceiling in this case being supported by eight small iron columns up to the cornice, immediately over those which support the Gallery.—

This construction will give to the ceiling a pleasant and elegant form.

The Basement of this Design, Plate XVI. should be stuccoed if not the whole of the Building.

PLATES XVII. XVIII. XIX. XX.

Plans, Section, and Elevation of a Design for a Chapel, on a large scale, size 100 feet by 64 feet: this will seat more than 2000 persons; of which I propose 200 to be free seats. A centre aisle might be made, if desired; in which case the side aisles should be next the walls.

Plate XVIII. shews the Plan of the principal Gallery, which is continued all round, with an extra depth to the Front Gallery. The organ is not intended to be placed in the situation shewn in the Plate, but in the upper Gallery. If the continuation of the Gallery across the eastern end should be objected to, it may be made to terminate at the walls, as is shewn by the dotted line; this I do not think would injure the effect, yet perhaps it would be better if the building were shortened.

A Section is shewn on Plate XIX. by which the situation of the upper Gallery is ascertained; the access to it by a staircase at the back of the front Gallery, marked Λ.

The Elevation, Plate XX. has a bold appearance, and should be stuccoed : the Pilasters may be of stone.

PLATES XXI. XXII.

Plan and Elevation for a Design for a Church, or Episcopal Chapel, 66 feet by 40 feet, exclusive of the Vestry, and is calculated to seat 600 persons, including 150 in the Gallery, at the end only.   I must observe, this Design was not made with the view of seating a great number of persons: it is more adapted for a place of worship on a gentleman's estate, or in his grounds.   The Elevation, Plate XXII. would have a good effect if it were stuccoed.

Estimate 2800*l.*

PLATES XXIII. XXIV.

Plan and Elevation of a Church in the Gothic style, size 70 feet by 40 feet, exclusive of the Tower and the Vestry.   This plan is calculated to seat 700 persons, of which I propose 200 to be free seats.   A Gallery at the end.

Plate XXIV. shews the Elevation, which exhibits a bold Tower, in the Gothic character.

PLATES XXV. XXVI. XXVII.

Ground Plan, Gallery Plan, and Elevation of a Design for a Church of the Grecian Doric Order; size 76 feet by 50 feet; calculated to seat 800 persons.   Estimate 6000*l.*

The Gallery Plan, Plate XXVI.   By this it will be seen, that there are only two ranges of Pews, those in the front forming good accommodations for the principal persons of the parish.

Plate XXVII. Elevation of the principal Front.

PLATES XXVIII. XXIX.

Design for a Church in the Gothic style, with a square Tower; the body of the Church in the interior is 66 feet by 44 feet; but the whole exterior of the Building is 95 feet by 49.   I propose to have Galleries on the sides behind the pillars, to which the handsome stairs in the front would lead, with an Orchestra at the end for the Organ.   To seat 700 persons. Estimate 7500*l.*

Plate XXIX.   Elevation of the Tower and Entrance Front. The nave being hid by this geometrical representation, destroys in a great degree the true effect of the building, which in perspective would be grand and imposing.

PLATES XXX. XXXI.

Plan and Elevation for a Gothic Church upon a large scale, with an octagon lantern Tower. The interior dimensions of the body of the Church 70 feet by 66 feet. The whole of the exterior will measure 110 feet by 72 feet. This plan will seat upwards of 1500 persons. Estimate 12,500*l*. The handsome vestibule entrance, with an enriched groined ceiling, and the noble staircases on each side, which lead to the Gallery, give to this Design a grand and noble effect suitable to the character of a wealthy and extensive parish. Here are also a number of free seats.

Plate XXXI. Elevation of the Tower Entrance and West Front.

PLATES XXXII. XXXIII. XXXIV.

Ground Plan and Elevations of a Design in the Grecian style, for a parochial Church. Interior dimensions, 75 feet by 50 feet, exclusive of the recess for the Altar; the whole of the exterior dimensions, 116 feet by 55. This Plan will accomodate 1200 persons, besides children, Estimate 12,500*l*.

A handsome flight of Steps leads to an Ionic Portico, which covers the entrance to the vestibule, which leads laterally to an appropriate staircase, each having a separate vestibule. The whole is thrown up on a suitable basement, and gives to this Design a good effect. Vaults for interment are proposed to be under the body of the Church.

Plate XXXIII. shews the side Elevation, with the lateral porticoes and entrances.

Plate XXXIV. Elevation of the West Front, with the Portico and Steeple.

PLATES XXXV. XXXVI.

Plan and Elevation of a circular Church, 120 feet in diameter, with three entrances. The circular range of columns contributes to support a spacious Dome springing from the entablature above, extending 80 feet in diameter, and rising 70 feet from the pavement to the summit of the vault. The area will receive light, principally, from the lantern in the centre of the Dome; the Gallery and the Aisles beneath, from the windows in the side walls. The centre area of the Church is proposed to be pewed, having aisles across, and a circular one under the Gallery, with free seats behind next the wall. The Organ to be placed immediately over the entrance from the front vestibule into the rotunda, and considerably above the level of the Gallery floor The steeple is 200 feet in height from the ground to the top of the cross. All the work above the blocking of the upper story is intended to be of copper and gilt. The order employed in the exterior of the Building is the Grecian Doric: in the interior the Ionic or Corinthian should be used.

I think the whole composition would, if well and judiciously executed in an advantageous situation, have a grand and imposing effect.

This Design would contain 2500 persons.

The Expense would not be short of 40,000*l.*

PLATE XXXVII.

Designs for two Towers.

PLATE XXXVIII.

Designs for two Towers.

PLATE XXXIX.

Designs for two Spires.

PLATE XL.

Designs for two Altar-pieces. That with Ionic columns is taken from one which I executed in a Church in Essex some years ago.

PLATE XLI.

Designs for two Altar-pieces. The upper one is that lately executed in Ranelagh Chapel. The arches over the windows are made in consequence of its situation. By turning to the Plan of the Edifice, Plate X. it will be seen that the Organ Gallery runs over it; the under side of which is thrown into groins; the whole together forming a very simple yet pleasing composition.

PLATE XLII.

Designs for two Altar-pieces.

PLATE XLIII.

Designs for two Pulpits. I must observe, that Pulpits partake of the nature of furniture; and, therefore, appear in a very different style from any part of a building. The one with columns is nearly the same as that executed in Ranelagh Chapel.

PLATE XLIV.

Two Designs for Pulpits. The Staircases to these must be accommodated to their situation.

THE END.

LONDON:

PRINTED BY JAMES MOYES,

Castle Street, Leicester Square.

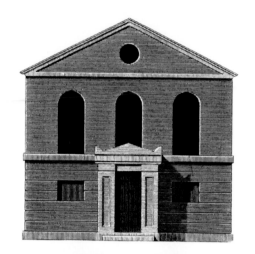

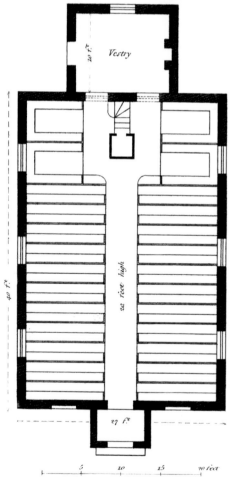

Vestry

22 feet high

5   10   15   20 feet

Plate 2

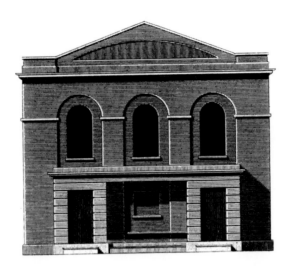

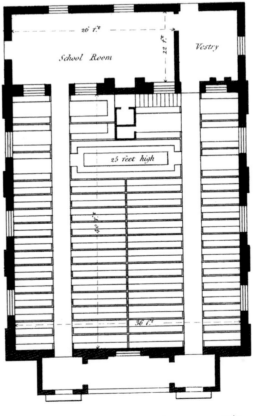

Plate 3

GROUND FLOOR PLAN.

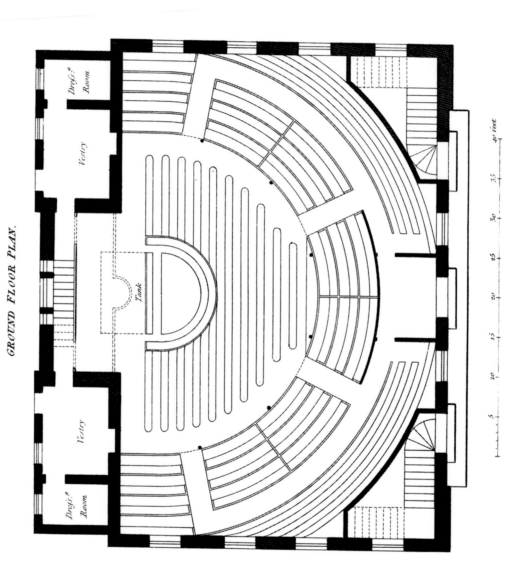

Dress.ᵍ Room

Vestry

Tank

Vestry

Dress.ᵍ Room

5   10   15   20   25   30   35   40 Feet

Plate 4.

GALLERY PLAN.

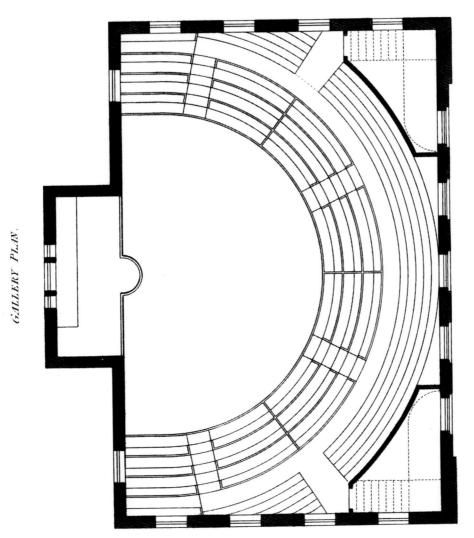

5 10 15 20 25 30 35 40 feet

Plate 5

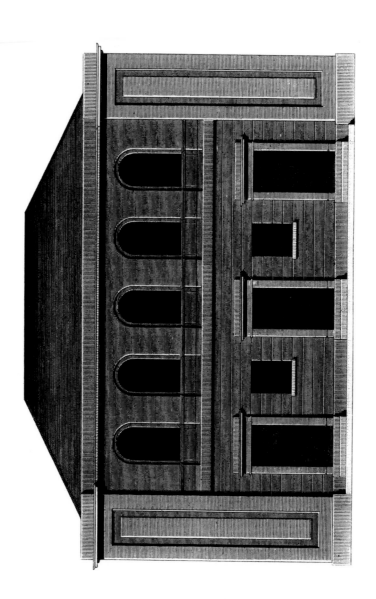

5 10 15 20 25 30 35 40 Feet

PLAN OF GROUND FLOOR.

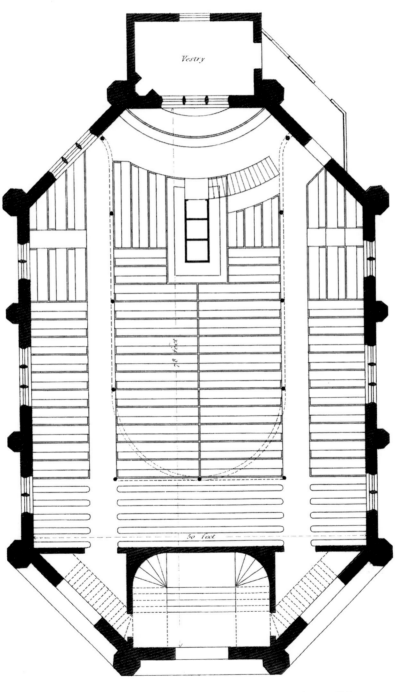

Plate 6

Vestry

78 feet

50 feet

5   0   5   10   15   20   25   30   35 feet

PLAN OF GALLERY.

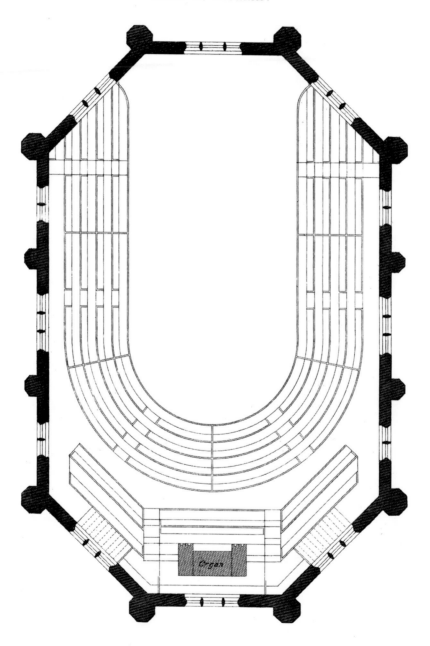

Organ

5   o   5   10   15   20   25   30   35 feet

Plate 8

5　10　15　20　25　30　35　40 Feet

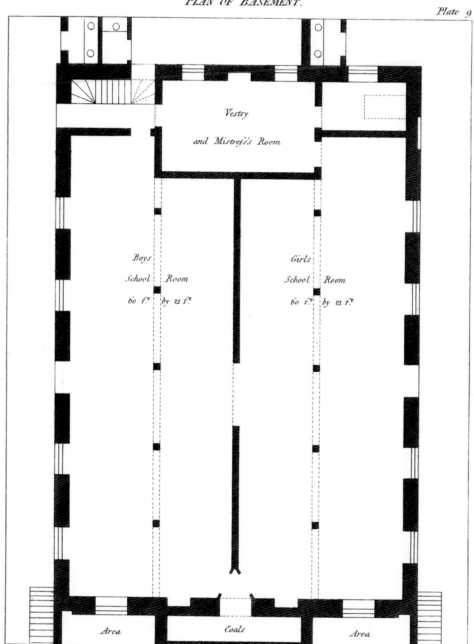

Vestry

and Mistress's Room

Boys
School Room
60 f.t by 21 f.t

Girls
School Room
60 f.t by 21 f.t

Area

Coals

Area

5   0   5   10   15   20   25 feet

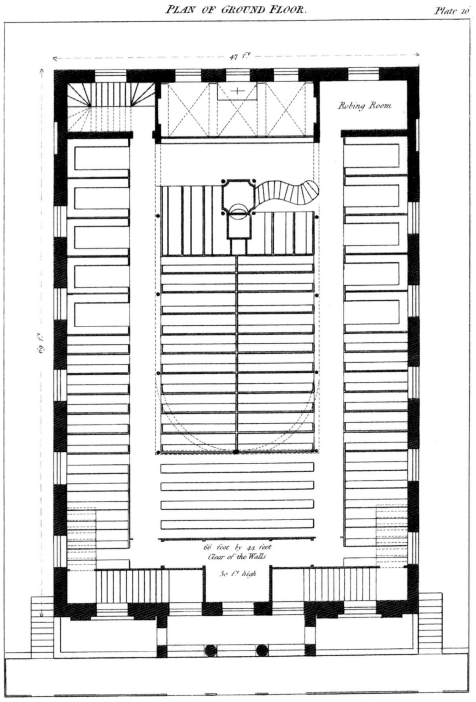

Robing Room

60 feet by 44 feet
Clear of the Walls

30 f.t high

47 f.t

60 f.t

5   0   5   10   15   20   25 feet

Plate II.

PLAN OF GALLERY.

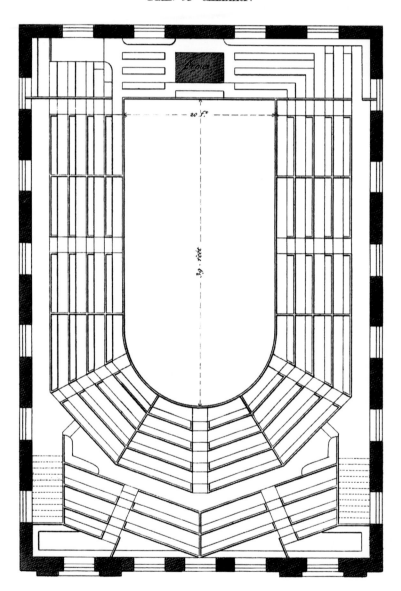

20 f.⁰

39 feet

5 .0 5 10 15 20 25 feet

Plate 22

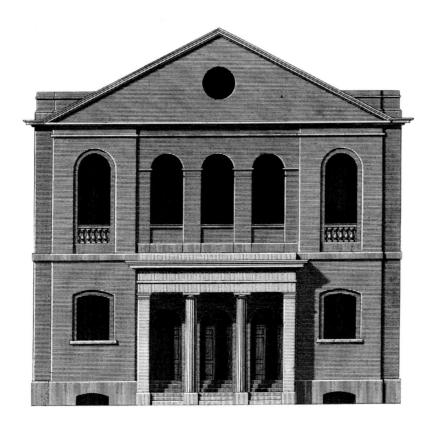

ELEVATION OF RANELAGH CHAPEL, CHELSEA.

5 0 5 10 15 20 25 feet

Plate 13

PLAN OF GROUND FLOOR.

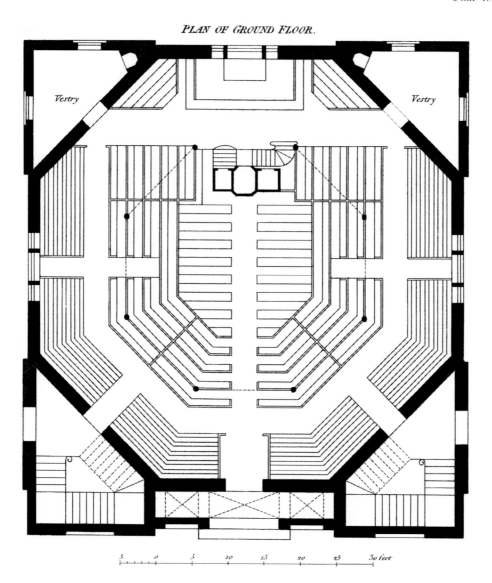

Vestry

Vestry

5   0   5   10   15   20   25   30 feet

PLAN OF GALLERY.

Plate 14

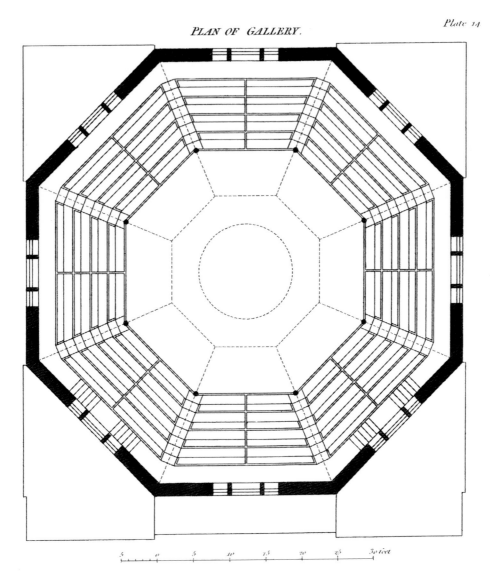

5   o   5   10   15   20   25   30 feet

Plate 15

SECTION.

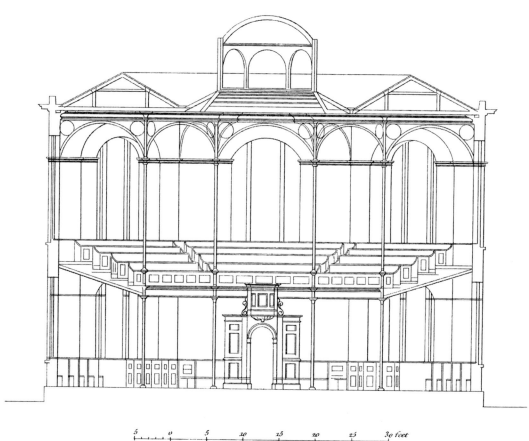

5 0 5 10 15 20 25 30 feet

Plate 16

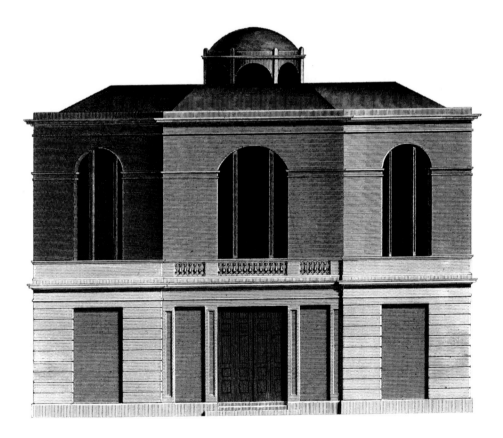

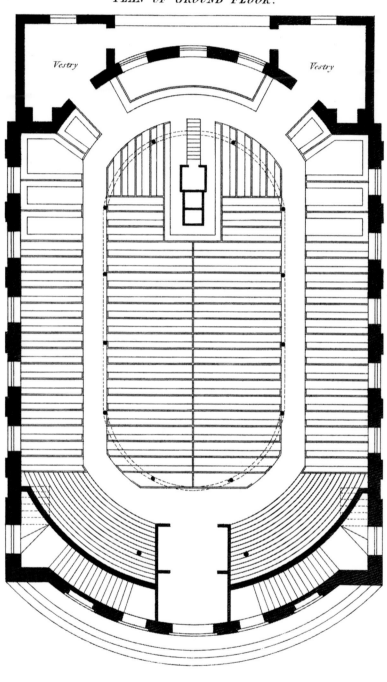

Vestry

Vestry

Plate 18

PLAN OF GALLERY.

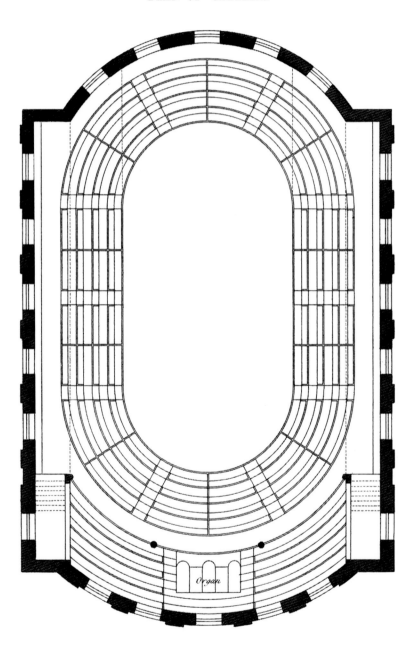

Organ

5   0   5   10   15   20   25   30   35   40   45 feet

Plate 19

SECTION.

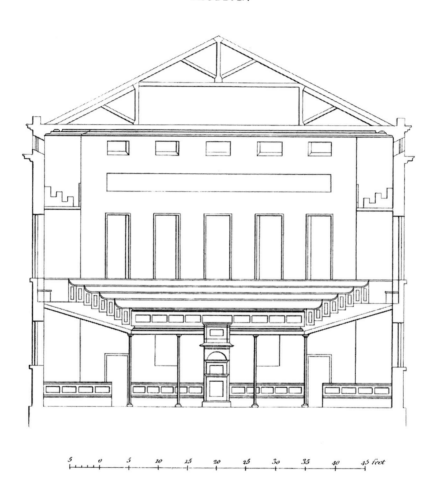

5   0   5   10   15   20   25   30   35   40   45 feet

Plate 20

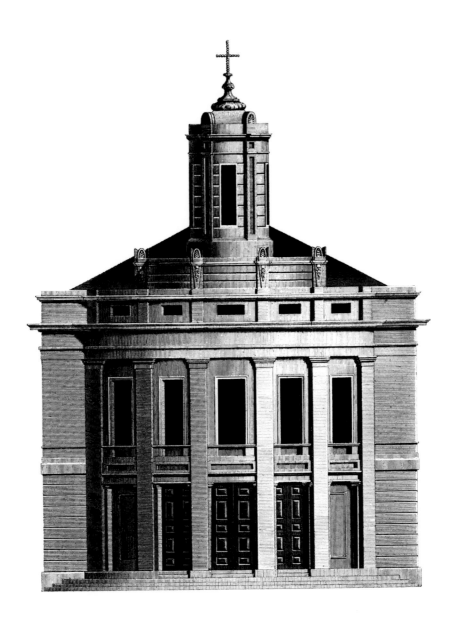

5   0   5   10   15   20   25   30   35   40   45 feet

Plate 21

GROUND PLAN.

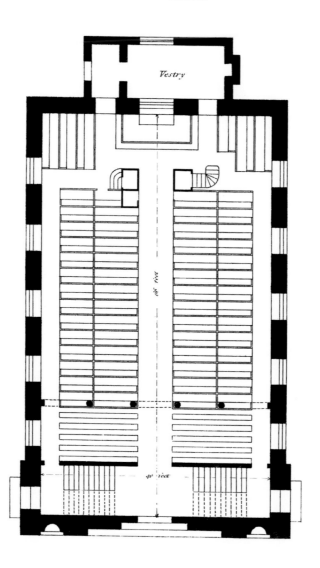

Vestry

5   0   5   10   15   20   25   30   35 feet

Plate 22

5   0   5   10   15   20   25   30   35 Feet

PLAN OF GROUND FLOOR.

Plate 23

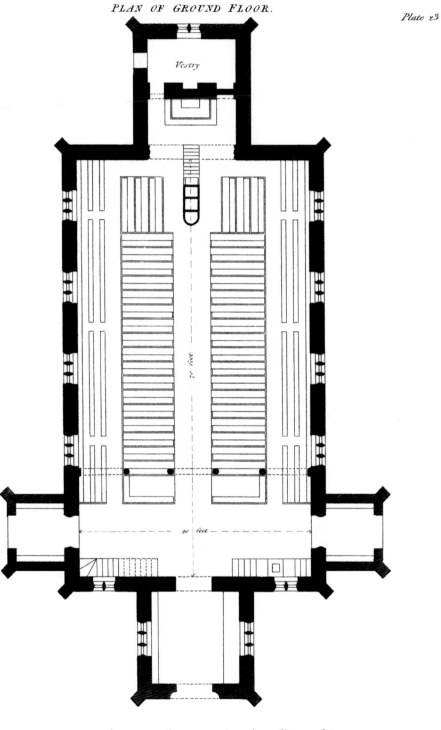

Vestry

Plate 21

Plate 25

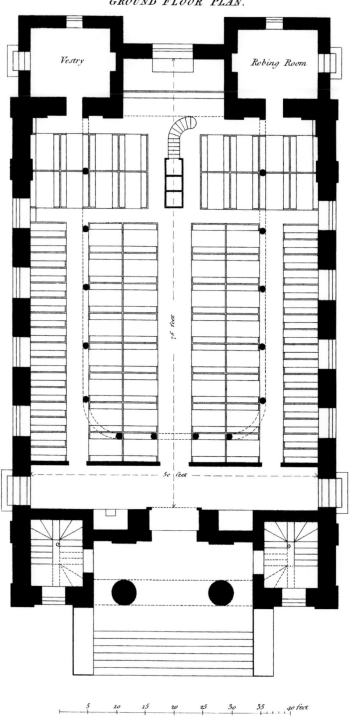

Vestry

Robing Room

5   10   15   20   25   30   35   40 feet

Plate 26

PLAN OF GALLERY.

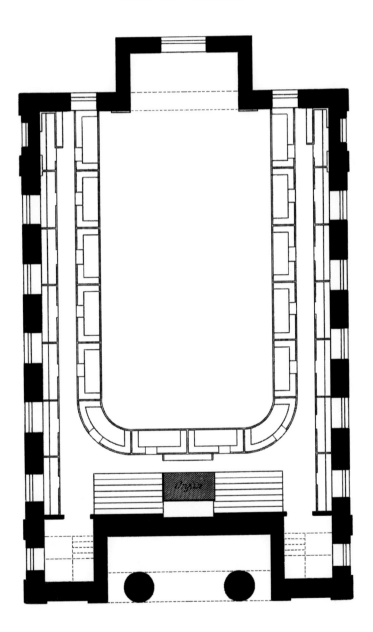

5   10   15   20   25   30   35   40 feet

Plate 27

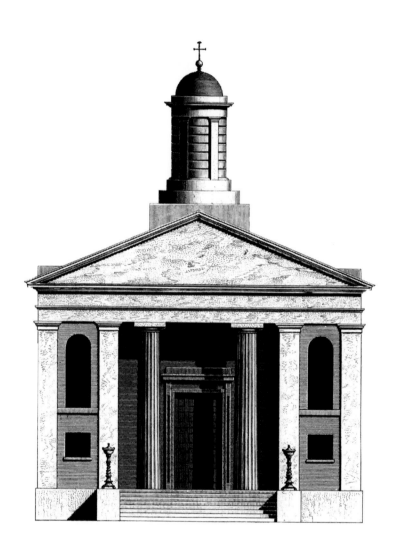

5   10   15   20   25   30   35   40 Feet

Plate 28

PLAN OF GROUND FLOOR.

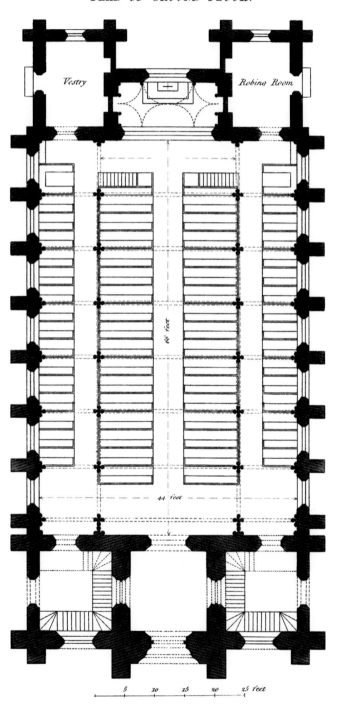

Vestry

Robing Room

60 feet

44 feet

5 10 15 20 25 feet

Plate 29

5   10   15   20   25 feet

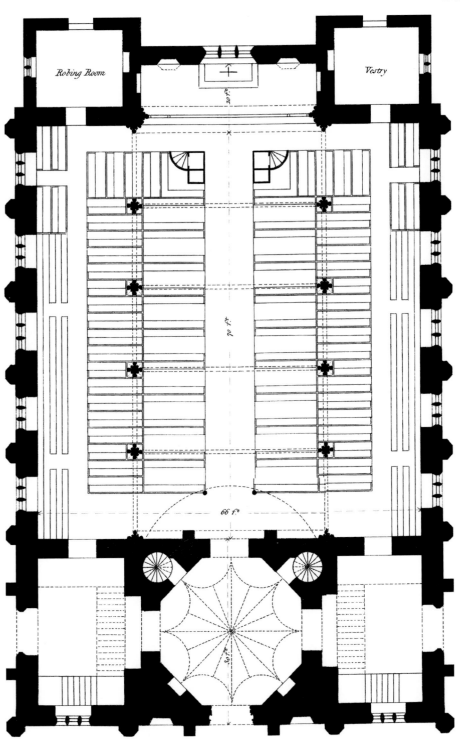

Plate 30

Robing Room

Vestry

66 f⁺

70 f⁺

5   10   15   20   25   30   35   40 Feet

Plate 31

Plate 32

PLAN OF GROUND FLOOR.

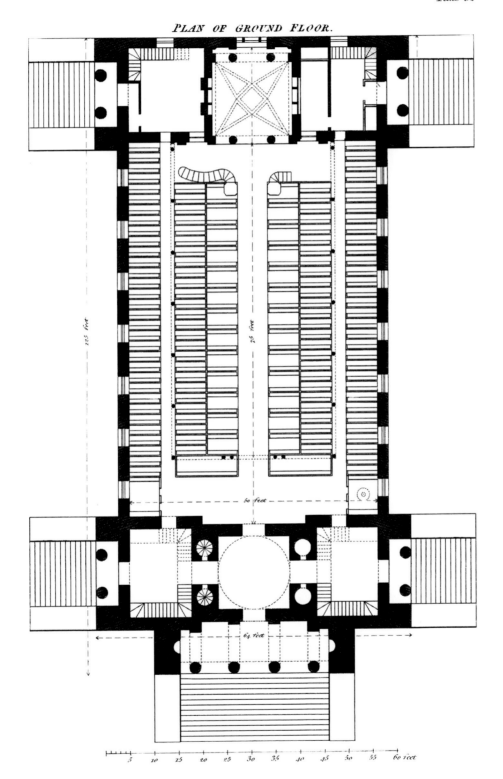

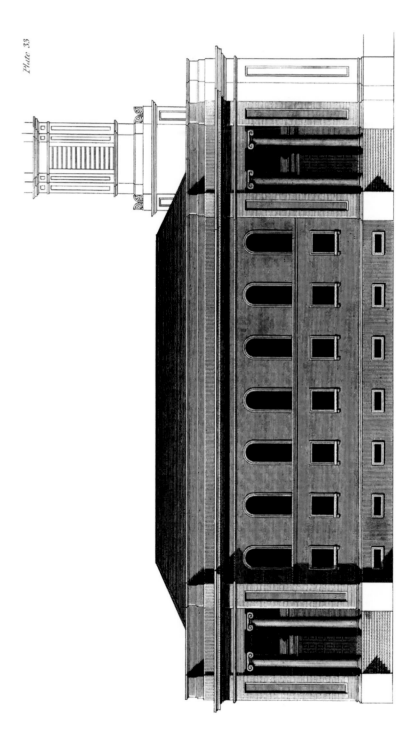

Plate 34

5   10   15   20   25   30   35   40   45   50   55   60 feet

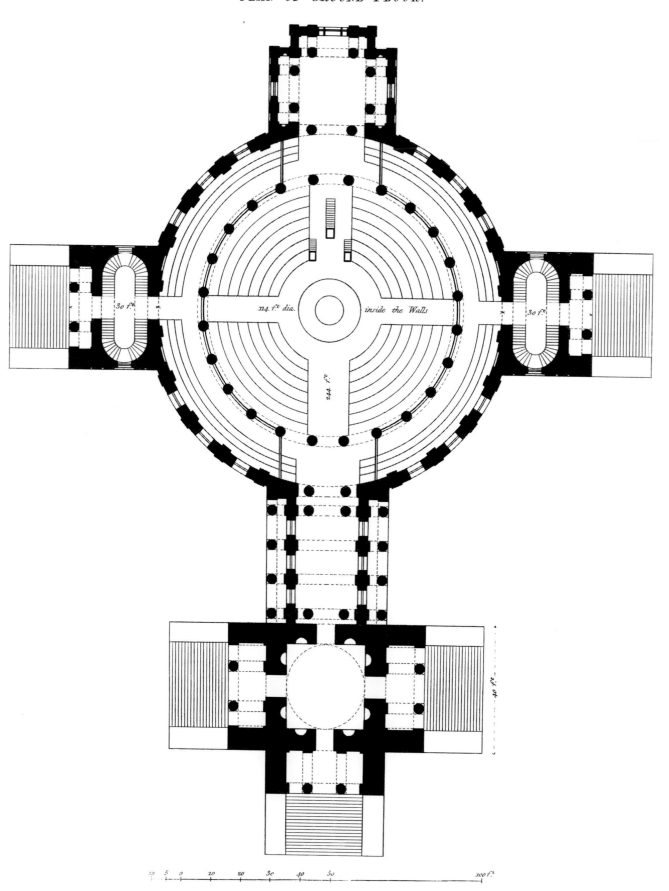

30 f.t

114 f.t dia.   inside the Walls

244 f.t

30 f.t

40 f.t

Plate 36

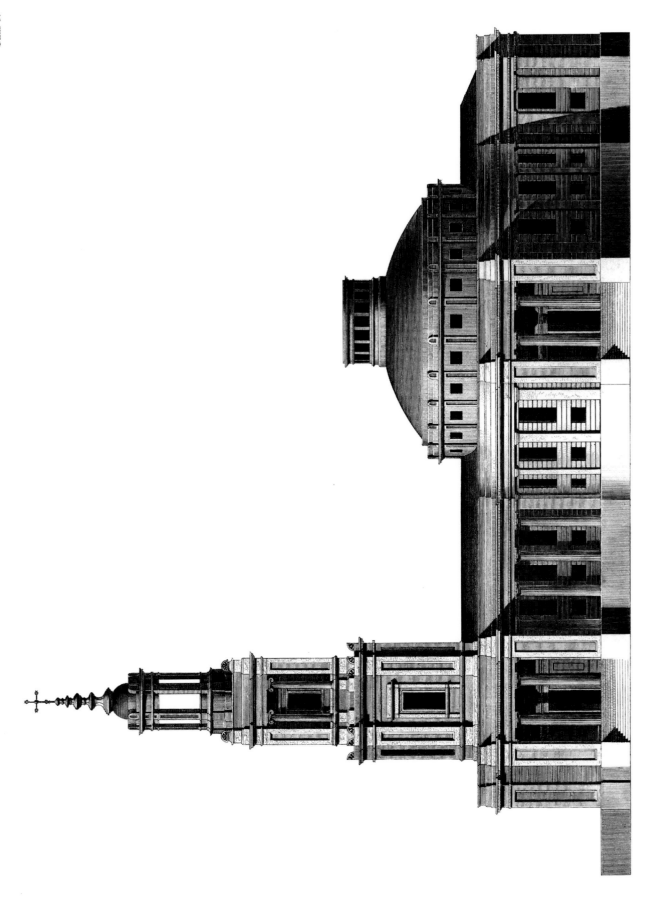

Plate 37

Plate 38

Plate 39

Plate 40

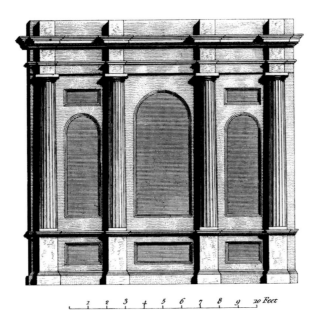

1 2 3 4 5 6 7 8 9 10 Feet

1 2 3 4 5 6 7 8 9 10 Feet

Plate 31

ALTARS.

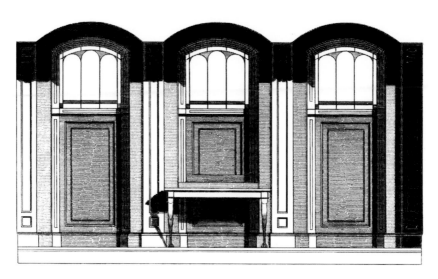

5   10 feet

1   2   3   4   5   6   7   8   9   10 feet

Plate 42

1 2 3 4 5 6 7 8 9 10 Feet

Plate 43

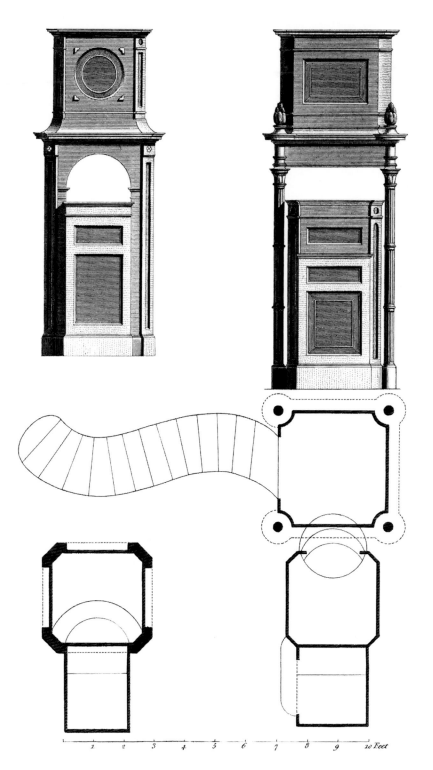

1   2   3   4   5   6   7   8   9   10 Feet

PLATE 44

PULPITS.